WE
PREACH

WE PREACH

THE PRIORITY AND PRACTICE OF APOSTOLIC PREACHING

JERRY JONES

WORD AFLAME PRESS
HAZELWOOD, MO

WORD AFLAME PRESS
8855 Dunn Road, Hazelwood, MO 63042
www.pentecostalpublishing.com

© 2016 by Jerry Jones

All rights reserved. No portion of this publication may be reproduced, stored in an electronic system, or transmitted in any form or by any means, electronic, mechanical, photocopy, recording, or otherwise, without the prior permission of Word Aflame Press. Brief quotations may be used in literary reviews.

All Scripture quotations in this book are from the King James Version of the Bible.

Printed in the United States of America

Cover design by Timothy Burk

Library of Congress Cataloging-in-Publication Data

Names: Jones, Jerry, 1952- author.
Title: We preach : the priority and practice of apostolic preaching / Jerry Jones.
Description: Hazelwood : Word Aflame Press, 2016. | Includes bibliographical references.
Identifiers: LCCN 2016033490 (print) | LCCN 2016033959 (ebook) | ISBN 9780757750441 (alk. paper) | ISBN 9780757750458 (spanish : alk. paper) | ISBN 9780757751974 () | ISBN 9780757751981 (Spanish)
Subjects: LCSH: Preaching.
Classification: LCC BV4211.3 .J656 2016 (print) | LCC BV4211.3 (ebook) | DDC 251--dc23

LC record available at https://lccn.loc.gov/2016033490

In memory of my pastor,
A. E. Carney, and with thanks to all those who gave
me
a chance to preach.

Contents

Foreword ix
Prologue xi
Part One – We Preach 1
   1. What Is Preaching? 5
   2. The Theology of Preaching 17
   3. Saved by Preaching 37
Part Two – The Preacher 53
   4. The Call to Preach 57
   5. The Preacher's Qualifications 67
   6. Preach the Word 79
Part Three – The Sermon: Preparation 93
   7. The First Steps to Preparing a Sermon 95
   8. What Type of Sermon Is It? 117
   9. Putting It All Together 137
Part Four – In the Pulpit: Presentation 191
   10. Getting and Keeping Attention 195
   11. The Anointing 215
Epilogue 231
Acknowledgments 235
Bibliography 237

Foreword

Once, when asked about writing, Saul Bellow said, "Well, I don't know exactly how it's done. I let it alone a good deal."

That's how I feel about preaching. I learned to preach by preaching. I let alone the theory behind it all. I learned what worked and what didn't by giving altar calls that brought no one to the altar, and more times than I care to remember watching people's eyes glaze over while I preached. The tradecraft of public speaking I learned by preaching revivals to crowds of thirty people (or less), revivals that started on Sunday night and went without break until the next Sunday night (with Sunday morning thrown in), then started up again the next Monday or Tuesday and went again until Sunday. They were long weeks if you "didn't connect." I learned to preach pastorally when I became a pastor and how to preach conferences and camps when I began to be asked to preach in those types of meetings.

I did not always understand the whys for things that I just knew to be so. Rhythm, cadence, and gauging the emotional impact of sermon points in order to find the most effective way of presenting them, along with a hundred other important things, were all more intuition than training. It was the theory I was lacking.

Then I began to be asked to teach sessions on preaching to aspiring preachers. For five years I taught a semester-long class on preaching at Gateway College of Evangelism. I discovered that people weren't really content to know that something is true just because I said it was. While they respected my experience, they wanted to know why it was so. I began to think about the mechanics of preaching. I wanted to discover why some things work and some don't. I also began researching what other preachers had to say about this calling and craft.

Now, I have written this book. In some ways it has been a joy, in others it has been a real challenge, one that has taken far too long to complete (just ask the editor). Part of the struggle is that I am still very much just a student of this fascinating collaboration between God and human beings, and suspect I always will be. But mainly, it is that the task of putting something you have learned by doing into not just words, but understandable and thus teachable words, has been a years-long commitment.

Now it's done, and I sure hope it helps somebody.

Prologue

We cannot be certain where the valley of dry bones was located, or what calamity had filled it with piles of human remains. Was this the site of some battle, and the bones the mingled remains of men who had once fought here? Or was it the place where the ill-fated migration of an entire tribe came to an end? We are given none of the details of how the bones came to be in this place. Maybe the message is that it doesn't matter: men and women arrive at the graveyards of their hopes by any number of pathways.

Into this scene of ruin and despair, God called a man, a human being, who by his own confession didn't have the answer to this dilemma of death. "Can these bones live?" was the question God asked this preacher. "Thou knowest," was the honest answer. Every preacher has been where this preacher was, called to a place in which he or she simply wasn't sure if anything could live.

"Can they live?" He looked over the valley full of scattered bones, nothing moving, the moan of the wind through empty ribcages the only sound. "Thou knowest," was the only possible answer.

Then came the directive, "Preach to them." It was a command and a promise all at once.

The command should not have been unexpected. After all, he was called to preach; it was his life's mission. Preaching is what preachers do. So he preached. "Oh, dry bones, hear the word of the Lord!" His words echoed across the silent valley as he preached to the dead. Probably at first there was no response; had a traveler happened to pass by he surely would have thought the preacher crazy. *Nobody is listening, nobody is responding.*

Then the impossible happens: there is movement in the valley. Of their own accord, bones begin to move almost as if by an invisible hand. Not randomly, but purposefully, the bones skitter across the desert floor, their mission at first a mystery, but soon plain enough: they are seeking their place, joining with bones from their former lives. Skeletons begin to take shape. Order is emerging from chaos: fingers to hands, hands to wrists, skulls to spines, until—under the power of preaching—lying across the desert are the outlines of human beings. Now sinew and flesh begin to appear, muscle and skin form over the bones until men are recognizable, until it seems they are almost alive.

Now the preacher falls silent. A miracle has occurred, the evidence lying at his feet, filling the valley floor. But what now? His preaching has effected a transformation beyond imagining, what power can now bring these to the next level? What can put breath into these lungs, life into these bodies?

"Preach to the wind!" comes the command.

With less hesitation and more anticipation, the preaching begins again: "Come from the four winds, oh breath, and enter into them!" And the breath comes, and those once dead, are made alive, and they rise to their feet. And where once there was only the stillness of death, now there is a mighty army, alive, strong, and ready to march.

Preaching still accomplishes miracles. Only preaching empowers a human being with one hand to reach into the world of human need and with the other into the world of divine power, and to pull those two worlds together.

This book is about this unique partnership between the human and the divine. It is not only a how-to book, although I hope you will find instruction and some down-to-earth help to improve your preaching, but it is more than that. It will explore the deeper and broader aspects of this incredible calling. We will not spend much time exploring the various types of preaching, evangelistic, homiletic, expository, and so forth, but will focus instead on techniques and principles that will improve your mastery of any type of preaching. We will linger on the three ingredients of persuasive public speaking, which are absolutely vital to understanding the human side of preaching. In doing so we will discuss these timeless principles in an era which prides itself in abandoning such principles, but is poor in offering anything to take their place.

Part One

We Preach

> For the Jews require a sign, and the Greeks seek after wisdom: But we preach . . .
>
> Paul

No matter what our station, daily life in a fallen world is a walk through a gauntlet of belittlement. Those who attend our churches are daily bombarded by false values and beliefs that cheapen God's creation, by personal slights and insults, by Satan's accusations. Their minds are assaulted by scabrous images in the media and by profanity that is objectionable to God precisely because it debases the creation. They are subject to sins that mar God's image within them. They suffer distorted images of themselves that distort God's truth.

After such a week, it's a wonder that a person can walk into church with any sense of worth. . . .

But then they hear anointed preaching, and gravity reverses as people sense the upward pull of heaven. The sermon reveals the character of God, who infuses all life with meaning and majesty. The sermon tells who we are in God's sight: created in the divine image, beloved beyond description, destined for glory. The sermon uncovers sins—then announces how to be redeemed. The sermon honors the morality that exalts humankind. The sermon assumes that people can think and discern about life and the Book of Life. The sermon appeals to the will, treating people as responsible agents whose choices matter forever. The sermon preaches Christ Immanuel, forever hallowing human flesh, second Adam who will one day resurrect believers in his likeness. A sermon is the most intense dose of dignity any person can receive.

Craig Bryan Larson

PART ONE

Before we get into how to preach better, let's talk about some of the fundamentals: What, exactly, is preaching? Why do we do preaching the way we do? Is preaching as we do it biblical, or is it just tradition? Does preaching have anything to do with salvation, or is it just one of those things we do to fill out a church service, no different from congregational singing, receiving an offering, or having a choir? It is important to answer these questions in order to know the value of this remarkable event.

1

WHAT IS PREACHING?

> Preaching is the communication of divine truth through human personality.
>
> Phillips Brooks

> A manifestation of the Incarnate Word, from the written Word, by the spoken word.
>
> Bernard Manning

What is preaching? Good question. Most of us have witnessed preaching nearly every week for most of our lives without giving much thought to what it really is. When we try to define preaching, it is surprising just how difficult it is to describe something so familiar. The definitions are many and varied. John Stott writes, "To expound Scripture is to open up the inspired text with such faithfulness and sensitivity that God's voice is heard and his people obey him." Jay Kesler defines it: "Preaching is distinguished from teaching in that it calls for commitment and attempts to bring people to a point of action." Andrew Blackwood defined preaching as "the truth of God voiced by a chosen personality to meet human needs."

In a series of lectures on preaching delivered at Yale University in 1877, Phillips Brooks gave what many consider the classic definition: "Preaching," he said in effect, "is the communication of divine truth through human personality." This is perhaps the best definition of preaching ever written because in a few words, it captures the fundamental ingredients that makes preaching more than simply public speaking. Here's what it tells us: *Preaching must contain divine truth.* Not the preacher's opinions, the latest pop culture slogans, the headlines from this morning's paper; it must communicate the timeless truth of God's Word. The preacher is not simply another voice competing with ten thousand other voices for our attention. It is not the entertainment value, the display of one's ability to persuade, or multimedia virtuosity that makes a sermon more than a speech. It is the content. Preaching deals in eternal truth.

Preaching must communicate truth. It must be presented so that people from all walks of life, all education levels, and all steps of spiritual development will grasp it and believe it and act upon its promise. Truth has power within itself. Nothing needs to be added to truth in order to set men and women free, change people's lives, or bring hope to any situation. It need only be clearly communicated for this power to be released into human lives.

And *preaching must come through human beings*. Not angels, nor robots, nor the lofty mountains or still afternoons of nature; it must come through humans. The personality of the preacher will and must shine through, and that personality is a vital component of the incredible thing called preaching. So preaching is truth communicated by a human being.

When you stop to think of it, this is a strange occurrence. A person standing alone before a crowd and proclaiming a message from God: it seems outlandish.

Preaching is not the choice of humankind; it is the choice of God. People may analyze its effectiveness, laugh at it, or declare it too old-fashioned to work in modern times, but preaching remains the choice of God. It will never lose its power nor fail to accomplish its purpose. Preaching is the audible voice of God. For the vast majority of us, preaching is the only divine voice we will ever hear. While the Lord often impresses hungry people with His words, that is, speaks to them within their spirits in a voice that only they can hear, God proclaims to all humanity His truth, His purpose, and His plan through the voice of the preacher.

It should not surprise us that preaching is the communication of divine truth through human personality. After all, the truth is not a collection of dry, arcane facts. The truth is a person who clearly proclaimed, "I am the Truth." To know this person, we must know both the person and the truth. Perhaps because He was and is a person,

He has chosen through the filter of human personality to proclaim Himself to the world.

Fads and fashions come and go, opinions and ideas shift like the sands of the Sahara, but the preaching of truth remains constant, unchanged. Each generation feels the need for something new, to find and proclaim a new way. The old ways fade and new ways take their place; this is so in almost every human endeavor. Even in the church, methods, ideas, fashions in dress, music, worship, visual presentation, architecture, and so many other things change. But there are some things that never change; there is a constant that connects each generation throughout the ages, and that constant is the preaching of the Word of God. From the Old Testament prophets through John the Baptist to the apostles, we find this common thread. We are on familiar ground when we read their sermons because they remind us of the experiences we have every Sunday when we join with our brothers and sisters and hear a preacher preach the gospel.

Preaching still appeals to the human heart. This is remarkable, not only because the act of preaching is thousands of years old, but also because it has, like most things religious, been the target of ever increasing attacks by anti-Christian movements, particularly in popular media and politics. Yet in spite of these efforts, it is estimated that between 130 and 150 million Americans go to church every week. This number means:

- More Americans gather in churches on any given weekend than gather in sports stadiums and arenas

to watch the games during the entire NFL, NBA, and NHL seasons combined.
- The major league baseball season lasts six months and includes 2,420 games, yet this Sunday more Americans will be in church than will attend every MLB game for the entire season.
- NASCAR is said to be the most attended sporting event in America based on average attendance per event, yet there will be more people in church on one Sunday than will attend all the NASCAR races for the next four years combined.
- It is thought that the Super Bowl is the most watched sporting event in the United States. Yet there will be more Americans in church this Sunday than will attend or watch the Super Bowl next February.
- The movies may be the most attended pastime in America with 1.27 *billion* tickets sold each year. Yet in just ten Sundays, more of us will be in church than will be at the movies for the whole year. In other words, more of us will be in church in the next year than will go to the movies for the next five years.

Most of those who go to church will hear some sort of preaching. Seen in that light, can we not say that listening to preachers preach is America's favorite pastime?

Preaching is central to Christianity because Christianity is a religion based on a particular book. The anointed preaching of that book—the Bible—is at the heart of all we do. In the United Pentecostal Church especially, preaching is the premier aspect of our worship. Our services are built around it. Our most popular meetings remain those that are given almost exclusively to preaching. Our conferences, even those at which we do business, highlight preaching. This echoes our commitment to the Word of God, a commitment which is based on a continuing recognition that preaching is an absolutely vital component in the ultimate salvation of a soul.

> For after that in the wisdom of God the world by wisdom knew not God, it pleased God by the foolishness of preaching to save them that believe. For the Jews require a sign, and the Greeks seek after wisdom: But we preach Christ crucified, unto the Jews a stumbling block, and unto the Greeks foolishness; But unto them which are called, both Jews and Greeks, Christ the power of God, and the wisdom of God (I Corinthians 1:21–24).

In society as a whole, the popularity of preaching, as well as that of preachers, has ebbed and flowed. In the early church, being a preacher was downright dangerous. Stephen was stoned, James was killed by the sword, and according to tradition, all the original apostles except one were martyred. Paul was beheaded. Of course, Constantine changed all that. During the collapse of the Roman Empire and the Dark Ages that followed, superstition shrouded preachers in mystery and turned them into more myth than men. The role of preaching ebbed and flowed during the passing centuries, and as it did, the state of preaching was an indication of the state of the church as a whole.

Brown, Clinard, and Northcutt in *Steps to the Sermon* discuss the link between preaching and the health of the church through two thousand years of church history:

> Whenever Christianity has made substantial progress, great preaching has led the way. In the history of Christianity there have been five great centuries of growth and development. These same five periods are the five centuries of great preaching: the first with the apostles, the fourth with Chrysostom and Augustine, the thirteenth with Francis of Assisi and Dominic, the sixteenth with Luther and Calvin, and the nineteenth with Spurgeon and Maclaren. Contrariwise, whenever preaching has declined, Christianity has become stagnant. In the Dark Ages, in the fourteenth and fifteenth centuries, and in the seventeenth and eighteenth centuries, in most countries, preaching was weak and ineffective.

It can be argued that the rapid growth, sustained enthusiasm, and strong appeal of the Pentecostal movement—and especially the United Pentecostal Church International—throughout the twentieth century are direct results of continuing emphasis on preaching. However, even in our churches, when other things begin to overshadow preaching, the church grows weak.

This is true simply because the power of God is unleashed by preaching the Word of God: "For the preaching of the cross is to them that perish foolishness; but unto us which are saved it is the power of God" (I Corinthians 1:18). To minimize preaching is to minimize the power of God. This is why churches often resort to entertainment, business theory, psychology, and a thousand other gimmicks to put people in the pew: there is no power where there is no preaching.

People still respond when the Word of God is preached. If you want to affect people's lives, preach the Word. If you want to build a great church, grow a great youth group, or have a great ministry, commit yourself to preach the Word. Fill your pulpit not with opinion, social commentary, jokes, pithy sayings, wit, impressive displays of education, and erudite philosophical speculation; rather, fill it with the Word of God. Preach the Bible and people will come, they will be changed, and your ministry will matter.

People are hungry for truth, for what is real. Sometimes we fail to distinguish reality from the everyday routine and the life situations we all live with. This is an error. This life is an illusion. Its details seem to matter, but they have only transitory meaning. We approach life as if it will last forever; as if education, success, or acceptance will endure, but they don't. The only real world is the world of the eternal; it is made up of those things that do indeed endure. To settle for the temporary when the eternal is within reach is the greatest tragedy of the human experience. Even those whose lives are little more than a steady diet of pop culture delivered by television, the movies, and the news cycles understand in their deepest thoughts that there surely is more to life than they have found. Alcoholism, drug abuse, and the mindless pursuit of unending pleasure are all symptoms of the search for purpose and meaning in life. Even the higher pursuits of life: culture, education, personal improvement, all ring hollow over time: "For after that . . . the world by wisdom knew not God" (I Corinthians 1:21).

This explains why 130 million Americans will attend church this Sunday, and most of them will hear preaching of some sort. Deep down, they understand that the answers to their questions are in the preached Word of God. Never has preaching mattered more, and never has true Bible preaching been needed more.

It has been said that asking a preacher to describe the ingredients of good preaching is like asking a cow to analyze milk. Preaching is most often produced without close examination of the process involved, and this is all right. But when we stop to analyze just what it is we do and how we do it, we find that while preaching is, of course, a spiritual event, it is also a skill that is rooted deeply in methods of communication that can be learned and improved.

Of course how we define preaching, while important, is not nearly so important as what God tells us preaching is. To find that out, we now turn to the Bible.

Sources Cited in Chapter 1

John Stott, "A Definition of Biblical Preaching" in Haddon Robinson and Craig Brian Larson, eds., *The Art and Craft of Biblical Preaching* (Grand Rapids: Zondervan, 2005).

Jay Kesler, "Overfed, Underchallenged" in Haddon Robinson and Craig Brian Larson, eds., *The Art and Craft of Biblical Preaching* (Grand Rapids: Zondervan, 2005).

Andrew Watterson Blackwood, *The Preparation of Sermons* (Nashville: Abingdon-Cokesbury, 1948).

Phillips Brooks, *Lectures On Preaching Delivered Before the Divinity School of Yale College in January and February, 1877* (New York: E. P. Dutton, 1878).

H. C. Brown, Jr., H. Gordon Clinard, Jesse J. Northcutt, *Steps to the Sermon* (Nashville: Broadman Press, 1963).

Statistics in Chapter 1

Frank Newport, "In U.S., Four in 10 Report Attending Church in Last Week," last modified December 24, 2013, accessed July 18, 2016, http://www.gallup.com.

Estimated attendance figures for sporting events and movies in recent years:

NFL 2014	17.4 million
NBA 2014–15	21.9 million
NHL 2013–14	22.3 million
MLB 2014	73.7 million
NASCAR 2013	3.5 million
Superbowl 2015	114.4 million viewers
Movies 2014	1.3 billion tickets sold
Churches 2015	6.8 billion (with an average of 130 million attending each Sunday)

http://www.statista.com/statistics/283897/national-football-league-teams-ranked-by-average-attendance-2013/
http://www.nba.com/2015/news/04/16/nba-sets-attendance-record-with-nearly-22-million-fans.ap/
http://www.hockeyattendance.com/league/nhl/
http://www.ballparksofbaseball.com/2010presentattendance.htm
https://www.quora.com/Why-is-NASCAR-attendance-down
http://www.nytimes.com/2016/02/09/sports/football/viewership-of-super-bowl-falls-short-of-record.html?_r=0
http://www.mpaa.org/wp-content/uploads/2015/03/MPAA-Theatrical-Market-Statistics-2014.pdf

2

THE THEOLOGY OF PREACHING

Preaching is not entertainment, nor is it an ego exercise for the preacher. It is not the result of tradition or old-fashioned communication methods that ought to be supplanted by more modern concepts and techniques. God chose preaching. Its beginning is rooted in the Bible. The word *preach* in one form or another occurs 153 times in Scripture. Seven times it is found in the book of Ecclesiastes where it is more a title than an action. That leaves 146 times. That puts *preaching* on par with words such as *hope* (156), *believe* (146), and *prayer* (144). Only four of the 146 mentions are in the Old Testament, but as we will see, it is rich with examples of preaching.

The New Testament has no formal definition of preaching. Instead it presents preaching by describing the preaching ministries of John the Baptist, Jesus, Peter, Paul, Stephen, and hinting at that of others. It is as if the writers took for granted that their readers were familiar with the concept and needed no more explanation of it. Because of this, it's fair to say that preaching was a common experience.

As heralds of the news of Jesus Christ and His resurrection, first-century preachers would have followed the long-settled techniques of orators and teachers, delivering their message with passion and effect. Their models would have been preachers and proclaimers in the Old Testament, as well as John the Baptist and Jesus Himself. It seems reasonable that the principles of persuasive rhetoric taught by the Greeks would have come into play. So we can consider three examples early apostolic preachers would have been influenced by: Old Testament prophesy and preaching, Greek oratory, and the preaching of Jesus and John. Before we look at each of these examples, let's consider how information was communicated in the time of the early church.

The ancient world was largely illiterate. Scholars differ in estimates, but the consensus seems to be that no more than 10 percent of the population was able to read. By illiterate, of course, we mean they could not read, not that they were unintelligent or uninformed. In fact, the ancient world transmitted information very effectively from person to person, between cultures, and across generations.

It is important to realize that reading in the ancient world was a hearing experience; that is, people read aloud for others to hear. Reading as a private, silent activity was unusual. Some scholars insist that ancient Greeks and Romans could not read silently because the lack of punctuation or even spacing between words, sentences, and paragraphs made it impossible. Lucretia Yaghjian encourages us to see ancient reading in a new way:

> If we are to understand reading in the cultural world of the NT, we must first take off the conceptual lenses through which we habitually read, and begin to read with our ears as well as our eyes. Second, we must change our societal image of reading from a private rendezvous with the printed page to a public broadcast of oral and/or written communication. Finally we must revise our culturally biased definitions of literacy and illiteracy and allow the biblical documents to spell out their own contextual ones.

The reader could have been reading from a text, like Ezra did at the Water Gate in Nehemiah 8, or the reader may have been reciting from memory, but the result for the hearer was the same. This was how almost everybody learned: by listening to a reader read or recite stories, proclamations, instructions, or the Word of God. When, in His sermon recorded in Matthew 5, Jesus repeatedly used the expression, "Ye have heard that it was said by them of old time," He was describing literally how people learned. This oral method of teaching and learning was universal and endured for thousands of years. Certainly, as Joanna Dewey asserts, "early Christianity was an oral phenomenon in a predominantly oral culture."

Old Testament Preaching

The first-century church was familiar with preaching through the example of Jewish Scripture and culture. Public reading of the Word of God was an integral part of Jewish life, and the powerful presentation of the Word was common. Oratory was part of the Jewish tradition.

The Old Testament is a rich record of preachers and preaching. The preachers of the early church were familiar with the preachers and sermons in the Old Testament. We know this from the many references to them in the New Testament. Jude quoted Enoch, the earliest preacher of whom we have record: "And Enoch also, the seventh from Adam, prophesied of these, saying, 'Behold, the Lord cometh with ten thousands of his saints, To execute judgment upon all, and to convince all that are ungodly among them of all their ungodly deeds which they have ungodly committed, and of all their hard speeches which ungodly sinners have spoken against him'" (Jude 1:14–15). Peter called Noah "a preacher of righteousness" (II Peter 2:5). In the dark time in which Noah lived, to preach righteousness could not have been a popular life work. The seemingly insignificant result of his preaching, the saving of only seven other people, must have been disappointing, but preach he did and saved humankind in the process.

Abraham was the first person in Scripture to be called a "prophet" (Genesis 20:7). The Hebrew word used there is *nabi* and means "one who tells forth, announces, proclaims." So it was understood early on that a true prophet was a preacher, God's mouthpiece, and spoke the words that God gave him.

It is ironic that Moses felt he was unable to speak for God in the courts of Pharaoh. Maybe he was insecure and self-consciously discounting his abilities, or maybe he grew into his calling over time, but either way, Moses became one of the great preachers of the Old Testament. James F. Stitzinger describes Moses' final words to Israel in Deuteronomy 31–33 as "one of the earliest examples of revelatory preaching. . . . This address was delivered with tremendous ability and clarity." David L. Larsen believes that the entire book of Deuteronomy is a series of sermons, culminating with Moses' farewell. So powerful is this book that when it was rediscovered in the time of Josiah, read by Shaphan, and interpreted and applied to their times by Huldah the prophetess, a great revival came to Judah. (See II Chronicles 34:14–33.) That Moses' preaching ministry was well-known in New Testament times is confirmed by Stephen's description of him in his sermon before the Sanhedrin: "And Moses was learned in all the wisdom of the Egyptians, and was mighty in words and in deeds" (Acts 7:22).

Joshua left two farewell sermons (Joshua 23:2–16; 24:2–27) that John A. Broadus says "are really quite remarkable . . . in their finely rhetorical use of historical narrative, animated dialogue, and imaginative and passionate appeal."

The prophets were preachers with extraordinary impact on their nation. They weren't just future tellers; they often called the people to repent and obey the Lord, and they powerfully proclaimed the Word of God. They preached with the purpose of getting a response from their hearers.

Through psalms, proverbs, accounts of visions and dreams, illustrations, metaphors, instruction, explanation, and personification, they proclaimed the Word as they were inspired of the Holy Spirit.

A well-known and dramatic example of preaching by an Old Testament prophet was the sermon Nathan preached in David's court. (See II Samuel 12.) David had fallen into adultery with Bathsheba, the wife of Uriah. When she became pregnant, he tried to hide his adultery by summoning Uriah home from battle, hoping he would spend the night with his wife, and thus disguise the fact that the child was conceived while Uriah was away. When Uriah refused to do so, declining special treatment unavailable to his fellow soldiers, David sent him back to battle and sent instructions to Joab to put Uriah in the most dangerous place on the battlefield. Uriah was killed, and the plot to hide David's sin seemed successful.

Then the Lord sent Nathan with a sermon for the king. Nathan preached that sermon using a parable designed specifically for David. It was the simple story of a poor man and his ewe lamb:

> There were two men in one city; the one rich, and the other poor. The rich man had exceeding many flocks and herds: But the poor man had nothing, save one little ewe lamb, which he had bought and nourished up: and it grew up together with him, and with his children; it did eat of his own meat, and drank of his own cup, and lay in his bosom, and was unto him as a daughter.

> And there came a traveller unto the rich man, and he spared to take of his own flock and of his own herd, to dress for the wayfaring man that was come unto him; but took the poor man's lamb, and dressed it for the man that was come to him (II Samuel 12:1b–4).

David, of course, had been a shepherd and the least among his brothers, so Nathan's choice of this parable was shrewdly designed to connect with the king on an emotional level. Nathan also obviously knew David's empathy for the underdog, as well as his sense of justice and fairness. All these were used to bring the king face-to-face with his sin. Nathan's courageous response when David indignantly pronounced judgment on the rich man in the story, "Thou art the man!" shattered David's facade and brought him to repentance. "I have sinned against the Lord!" the king cried. Although not released from the consequences of his sin, David repented and was forgiven.

The rich legacy of effective and inspired preaching in the Old Testament was the background for the ministries of John and Jesus and the first-century church. This was their context for understanding exactly what preaching was.

Greek Oratorical Tradition

First-century Christians were not only well aware of the Old Testament examples of preaching, but they were also part of a culture steeped in oratory. When Alexander the Great swept through the known world in the fourth century BC, he conquered not only kings and kingdoms, but also minds and cultures. Greek language, thought, and culture began a reign that resisted Roman conquest and even the rise of Christianity. Greek rules of rhetoric, later joined by Roman thought on the subject, became the standard for all public speaking.

Some scholars have identified the first formulation of the rules of rhetoric with Korax about 466 BC. Korax taught that five parts of a speech were needed to make an effective, persuasive argument: introduction, presentation of facts, argument, secondary remarks, and closing. Later, Aristotle's teachings on rhetoric became deeply rooted in the ancient culture. His descriptions of persuasive rhetoric remain classic. He taught that only three technical means of persuasion are possible: the speaker must prove his case by appealing to (a) the character of the speaker, (b) the emotions of the hearer, and/or (c) traditional proofs, such as statements of experts or the merits of the argument itself. His suggested use of what he called *ethos* (character of the speaker), *pathos* (emotions inspired in the hearers), and *logos* (the persuasiveness of the speech as judged by the hearers), form the core of Greco-Roman rhetoric. Aristotle's influence was immense. Even today we see the influence of his teaching. In books on preaching we read that every sermon consists of three parts: for example, the preacher, the presentation, and the preparation; in other words, ethos, pathos, and logos.

It is beyond the scope of this chapter to examine Greco-Roman rhetoric in detail, but we cannot discount its influence on how the first-century church would have understood the act of preaching.

New Testament Preaching

The first-century church not only had the examples of Old Testament preaching and Greco-Roman oratory, but the ministries of John and Jesus were fresh in their minds. The Messiah and His forerunner were not ordinary men, nor were they ordinary preachers. They stirred an entire nation, indeed changed the world, and while Jesus' death, burial, and resurrection were the heart of this change, preaching was the centerpiece of their ministries.

John was a remarkable character and a fearless preacher. His confrontational style brought crowds of people to hear him preach, including the Pharisees and Sadducees, whom John denounced as a "generation of vipers" (Matthew 3:7). He was a true forerunner, making the way for the One who would come after. Preaching outdoors to huge crowds, he was a rough-hewn man whose sermons stirred his listeners to action. They repented, confessed their sins, and obeyed his call to baptism. He also inspired others to follow him, preparing them as individuals for later encounters with Jesus, and even later ministries of their own. We know Andrew and John, probably along with Andrew's brother Simon (later nicknamed Peter by Jesus) and John's brother James, were disciples of John before they answered Jesus' call to "follow me."

Matthew preserved enough of John's preaching to give us the flavor of his passionate and powerful delivery:

> O generation of vipers, who hath warned you to flee from the wrath to come? Bring forth therefore fruits meet for repentance: And think

not to say within yourselves, "We have Abraham to our father:" for I say unto you, that God is able of these stones to raise up children unto Abraham. And now also the axe is laid unto the root of the trees: therefore, every tree which bringeth not forth good fruit is hewn down, and cast into the fire. I indeed baptize you with water unto repentance: but he that cometh after me is mightier than I, whose shoes I am not worthy to bear: he shall baptize you with the Holy Ghost, and with fire: Whose fan is in his hand, and he will thoroughly purge his floor, and gather his wheat into the garner; but he will burn up the chaff with unquenchable fire (Matthew 3:7b–12).

It is no wonder that when he turned his attention and tongue toward King Herod and Queen Herodias, he lost his head. Jesus gave him this tribute: "For I say unto you, among those that are born of women there is not a greater prophet than John the Baptist" (Luke 7:28).

Jesus' ministry began in a synagogue where He followed what had become the usual method of presenting the Word of God. In each synagogue there was a rostrum, or podium, that faced the congregation. Here reading, teaching, and preaching happened. In a service at the synagogue in His hometown, Nazareth, Jesus announced His ministry in a dramatic way:

And he came to Nazareth, where he had been brought up: and, as his custom was, he went into

> the synagogue on the sabbath day, and stood up for to read. And there was delivered unto him the book of the prophet Esaias. And when he had opened the book, he found the place where it was written, The Spirit of the Lord is upon me, because he hath anointed me to preach the gospel to the poor; he hath sent me to heal the brokenhearted, to preach deliverance to the captives, and recovering of sight to the blind, to set at liberty them that are bruised, To preach the acceptable year of the Lord. And he closed the book, and he gave it again to the minister, and sat down. And the eyes of all them that were in the synagogue were fastened on him (Luke 4:16–20).

Jesus commanded the attention of everyone there with His reading of this dramatic text, and then began His sermon simply, but powerfully: "This day is this scripture fulfilled in your ears" (Luke 4:21). The reaction of the people at first was amazement at the words of Jesus, and then turned to rage when the sermon challenged them to see Him as more than the local carpenter's son. This reaction would be echoed again and again in the preaching ministry of Jesus.

Jesus was in every sense a preacher. Mark introduced Him: "Now after that John was put in prison, Jesus came into Galilee, preaching the gospel of the kingdom of God, And saying, 'The time is fulfilled, and the kingdom of God is at hand: repent ye, and believe the gospel'" (Mark 1:14–15). He preached and taught to huge crowds, delivering remarkable sermons that continue to connect with those who read them today. He preached with passion and conviction. He modeled proclamation of the gospel for all time.

Preaching in the Early Church

By studying these three examples of preaching and recognizing they would have formed the early church's understanding of preaching, we can begin to glimpse what first-century preaching would have looked and sounded like. The first Pentecostal preachers would have modeled their preaching after the preachers of the Old Testament, added proven techniques of rhetoric that were on display everywhere in the culture, and followed the examples of John and Jesus.

We can also learn what early preaching was like by examining how the authors of the New Testament used various words to discuss and describe preaching. Wolfgang Friedrich in the *Theological Dictionary of the New Testament* identifies thirty-three different verbs in the New Testament that describe the act of preaching. We will not cover them all since I don't want to bore you; moreover, most of them play a minor role in describing preaching, so we will only look at three of the most important.

κηρύσσω *(kerysso)*

Kerysso is the most common verb used for preaching in the New Testament, and it means "to proclaim" or "to herald." It is used to describe the preaching ministries of John the Baptist in Mark 1:4, of Jesus in Mark 1:14, and of the apostles in Mark 3:14. It pictures a herald who is sent to proclaim the occurrence or explanation of an event. The word is thought to come from the Old Persian word, *xrausa*, which, according to Klaas Runia in a 1977 lecture entitled "What is Preaching According to the New Testament?" means "to cry out loud and clear." In Greek usage outside the New Testament, an interesting example is the use of the verb by the great Roman historian Plutarch. In 197 BC a herald named Flaminius appeared at the Isthmian Games in Greece to announce the Roman victory over the Macedonians in a recent battle. Runia describes the importance of this example: "At the same time [he announced the Roman victory], Flaminius also announced the liberty and autonomy of Greece. The two facts were connected. At the moment that Flaminius announced the victory, the Greeks virtually became free. By his 'proclamation' he, as it were, set an [already] existing fact into motion."

So κηρύσσω (kerysso) has a twofold meaning. It not only means the proclamation of an event, but also the effect of that event on the listener. Runia explains it like this: "In the act of the κηρύσσειν [proclaiming] the event becomes reality for the listener."

Of course, the mere proclamation itself does not produce this effect on the listener. The content of the message is vital to the result. Friedrich says: "The essential point about the report which [heralds] give is that it does not originate with them. Behind it stands a higher power. The herald does not express his own views. He is the spokesman for his master. . . . Heralds adopt the mind of those who commission them." Important for our purposes, the New

Testament stresses the importance both of the content preached and its proclamation. Without proclamation, the essential content of the gospel will never reach its intended audience. According to Friedrich the verb *kerysso* occurs sixty-one times in the New Testament, while the noun *kerygma* occurs only eight times. This leads Friedrich to comment: "Emphasis does not attach to the [*kerygma*]. . . . The decisive thing is the action, the proclamation itself. . . . The divine intervention takes place through the proclamation." Runia says it like this: "wherever this event is proclaimed, it inaugurates what this event has accomplished. The new situation, brought about by the death and resurrection of Jesus Christ, now becomes reality for every listener who accepts it in faith."

How does the New Testament writers' use of this verb reflect the way the first-century church thought about preaching? Friedrich asserts that "preach" does not adequately convey the full meaning of *kerysso* in New Testament usage. *Kerysso* "does not mean the delivery of a learned and edifying . . . discourse in well-chosen words and a pleasant voice. It is the declaration of an event." Friedrich leaves no doubt as to what preaching accomplishes and how it does so: "Christian preaching does not persuade the hearers by beautiful and clever words—otherwise it would only be a matter of words. Preaching does more. It takes place in the spirit and in power."

εὐαγγελίζω (*euangelizo*)

Euangelizo occurs fifty-four times in the New Testament and means the same thing as *kerysso*, that is "to preach."

However, *euangelizo* carries with it the added emphasis that the message that is preached is the good news of the gospel, that is the death, burial, and resurrection of Jesus. The important thing to remember is that there is no implication that saving power is in the simple understanding of the historical fact. Unless it is preached, no *evangelizing* (an English word that comes from *euangelizo*) takes place. When united with the power of Spirit-anointed preaching as it is intended to be, proclaiming the good news of the gospel is effective, bringing demonstration and power, ministering to the whole gamut of human need. As Friedrich writes, *euangelizo* "is not just speaking and preaching; it is proclamation with full authority and power. Signs and wonders accompany the evangelical message. They belong together, for the Word is powerful and effective."

μαρτυρέω (*martyreo*)

The third verb we will look at is *martyreo*. It means "to witness." The noun form μάρτυς (*martys*) means "witness" or "one who testifies what he or she has personally seen or heard." Luke used the noun at the close of his Gospel to report the words of Jesus to the apostles:

> Then opened he their understanding, that they might understand the scriptures, And said unto them, Thus it is written, and thus it behoved Christ to suffer, and to rise from the dead the third day: And that repentance and remission of sins should be preached in his name among all nations, beginning at Jerusalem.

> And ye are witnesses of these things. And, behold, I send the promise of my Father upon you: but tarry ye in the city of Jerusalem, until ye be endued with power from on high (Luke 24:45–49).

The same description is found in Jesus' last words to His disciples: "But ye shall receive power, after that the Holy Ghost is come upon you: and ye shall be witnesses unto me both in Jerusalem, and in all Judaea, and in Samaria, and unto the uttermost part of the earth" (Acts 1:8). The power to accomplish this is in the Holy Spirit. God's power will enable them to fulfill the commission Jesus is giving them.

This is how we can be witnesses even though we were not there as the disciples were during those momentous days when Jesus was on the earth. Because of our faith and obedience and the empowerment of the Holy Spirit, we don't need to have personally seen the death, burial, and resurrection to be a witness of them. Neither is it necessary to have been in the number that heard Jesus declare that they would be witnesses (Acts 1:8). Both Paul and Stephen are called witnesses, although there is no evidence either of them ever met Jesus (outside of visions).

So what do we learn from this brief examination of the New Testament's three most commonly used terms to describe preaching? First, we learn that preachers are heralds of the good news of the death, burial, and resurrection of Jesus Christ. As heralds, they are proclaimers, not of messages of their own invention or choosing, but that of their Master. The New Testament focuses on the act of proclamation, but never loses sight of the content that must be proclaimed, so we must always see the message and its proclamation in tandem, not one without the other. By the proclamation of the gospel, those who hear and obey are saved, thus making not only the message but the proclamation itself a vital part of the process of salvation. Second, we learn that the message of the gospel is good news, not ignoring the tragic judgment that will come to all who reject it, but focusing on the opportunity for salvation for all who accept it. Third, heralds are not hirelings, but participants in this gospel. They are witnesses of its effectiveness by its work in their lives through their own faith and obedience. They are empowered by the Holy Spirit, which makes them ambassadors for God as they lift His words beyond those of human wisdom, and He infuses them with demonstration and power.

From what we have seen, it is clear that when the first-century church thought of communicating the gospel, they envisioned public proclamation. This was what the Old Testament demonstrated to them; it was what they were taught by Greek and Roman culture; it is what they witnessed in the synagogue, on city streets, and in the countryside; and it was the example of John the Baptist and Jesus. In an almost exclusively oral culture, public proclamation was the most common and effective way of communicating with the masses, and it was a part of daily life.

For first-century Christians, preaching was an event marked with divine power and carried out in a public setting. Preaching challenged the hearer with the gospel, produced conviction, and called for a response. It was preaching like Peter did on the day of Pentecost that came to model the presentation of the good news. Thousands responded to his sermon, and through its proclamation of the death, burial, and resurrection of Jesus, the church began with a remarkable explosion of growth. In the early years of the church, this kind of preaching was *the* method of propagating the gospel. In fact, some believe that much of the New Testament itself was first communicated as preached sermons. Klaas Runia asserts: "Form-critical research has, I believe, shown convincingly that much of the material which we now have in the gospels, originally, in the period of oral transmission, was passed on in the preaching of the early church."

So we conclude that, for the apostles, the method of presenting the gospel was verbal, usually in a structured setting, and that the form of the presentation was proclamation. This, to them, was preaching. It turned the world upside down, broke through barriers of paganism and persecution, and conquered the Roman Empire. Why would we abandon such a powerful tool today? Preaching is still God's method for proclaiming the gospel and, as in the first century, this means persuasive, passionate, and powerful proclamation. Let us preach as they did; I believe it will, even today, produce the same result.

Sources Cited in Chapter 2

Lucretia Yaghjian, "Ancient Reading" in Richard Rohrbaugh ed., *The Social Sciences and New Testament Interpretation* (Peabody, MA: Hendrickson, 1996).

Joanna Dewey, "Textuality in an Oral Culture: A Survey of the Pauline Traditions" in Joanna Dewey and Elizabeth Struthers Malbon, eds., *Orality and Textuality in Early Christian Literature* (Atlanta: Scholars Press, 1994).

James F. Stitzinger, "The History of Expository Preaching" in John McArthur, Jr.; Richard L. Mayhue; Robert L. Thomas, eds. *Rediscovering Expository Preaching* (Dallas: Word Publishing, 1992).

David L. Larsen, *The Company of the Preachers: A History of Biblical Preaching from the Old Testament to the Modern Era* (Grand Rapids: Kregel Academic & Professional, 1998).

John A. Broadus, *Lectures On the History of Preaching* (New York: Sheldon, 1886).

E. C. Dargan, *A History of Preaching* (New York: George H. Doran Co., 1905)

Wolfgang Friedrich, "Preaching" in Gerhard Kittel, Gerhard Friedrich, eds., Geoffrey W. Bromiley trans., *Theological Dictionary of the New Testament* (Grand Rapids: Eerdmans, 1964–76).

Klaas Runia, "What is Preaching According to the New Testament?" The Tyndale Biblical Theology Lecture for 1976, delivered at the School of Oriental and African Studies, London, on January 4, 1977.

3

Saved by Preaching

The purpose of preaching must always be the first condition that decrees its character. The final cause is that which really shapes everything's life. And what is preaching for? The answer comes without hesitation. It is for men's salvation.

Phillips Brooks

The central purpose of evangelical preaching is to win an immediate commitment to Jesus Christ.

Alan Walker

Some years ago, the church in Metairie, Louisiana, was involved in an extensive remodeling program. They were tearing down a portion of the old auditorium in preparation for a planned expansion that would substantially enlarge their church. In the portion of the construction that required demolition, there were some things they were not going to use after the project was finished, so they were not particular about moving them until it was necessary. One of those things was the old pulpit, which still sat in its usual spot.

One day they were taking down some of the rafters and lowering them carefully to the floor. Several men were on scaffolding high above the floor of the old auditorium. One of them, Ken Broussard, had the job of guiding down each rafter, once it was torn loose, to other men waiting below. He was standing twenty, twenty-five feet, maybe even more off the floor of the old auditorium, helping pass the rafters down. One of the long, heavy pieces of wood was lowered down to him, and at the moment he gripped it, the rafter slipped from the grasp of those above. The entire weight of the beam was on him. He knew he could not hold it alone, but in order to help protect those below him, he attempted to slow its fall until others could rush to help secure it. As he felt the weight, he took two or three steps back to try to balance himself, and Ken Broussard stepped backward, off the scaffolding, and into thin air.

Time seemed to slow as he fell. He realized that the distance of the fall was certainly enough to cause serious injury, maybe even enough to kill. Turning his head, he looked down, and beneath him he saw that the pulpit was still where it had stood for many years. When he saw it, he thought, *The pulpit is still on the old platform. That makes it several feet higher than the floor. If I could just fall on the pulpit, it would break my fall and maybe save me.* Somehow, he was able to twist in mid-air, turning completely over, and fell across the old pulpit. He rolled off the pulpit and onto the platform floor as men ran to him, alarmed, sure he was hurt, hoping they could help. His pastor ran to him and anxiously asked, "Brother Ken, are you all right?" Ken Broussard stood up, dusted himself off, and looked at the pastor.

"Yes, Pastor, I'm fine," he said. "I was saved by the pulpit."

All of us who have been born again were saved by the pulpit.

You preach to those that are lost. They are the slaves of sin, victims of its deception, entrapped by the call of the world. They are ruled by fear, doubt, hurt, worry. But preaching changes all of that. It liberates, frees, changes, empowers. It produces new hope, new confidence, new life. No wonder Paul said: "For the preaching of the cross is to them that perish foolishness; but unto us which are saved it is the power of God" (I Corinthians 1:18). Without a preacher preaching the Word, the process that leads to salvation is aborted before it is even begun.

In chapter 2 we gained a better idea of how preaching was understood by first-century Christians and presented in the New Testament. Now, let's look in more detail at its role in salvation. The role of preaching in the New Testament may be best described by Paul in Romans 10:12–15. In making the point that salvation is available to all, Jew and Gentile alike, he described a progression, in reverse, that takes a person from ignorance of the gospel to salvation:

> For there is no difference between the Jew and the Greek: for the same Lord over all is rich unto all that call upon him. For whosoever shall call upon the name of the Lord shall be saved. How then shall they call on him in whom they have not believed? and how shall they believe in him of whom they have not heard? and how shall they hear without a preacher? And how shall they preach, except they be sent? as it is written, How beautiful are the feet of them that preach the gospel of peace, and bring glad tidings of good things! (Romans 10:12–15).

Obviously, this passage illuminates the role of preaching in salvation, because the series of rhetorical questions that Paul asked leaves little doubt that without preaching, the chain—from hearing, to believing, to calling on the name of the Lord, to being saved—is not only broken, it remains unforged at all.

When Paul wrote his epistle to the Roman church, he had never been there. But many of its members were known to him. In fact, in the last chapter of the letter, he personally greeted twenty-six people, which William Barclay notes is far more than any other epistle. The majority of the saints in Rome were Gentiles, mostly freed men and women and slaves. There was also a significant Jewish minority. Since half of the names Paul mentioned in the letter are Jewish, perhaps Paul was a bit more familiar with the Jewish minority than the Gentile majority; at any rate he wrote with both in mind.

Salvation

The theme of Romans is found in 1:16–17: "For I am not ashamed of the gospel of Christ: for it is the power of God unto salvation to every one that believeth; to the Jew first, and also to the Greek. For therein is the righteousness of God revealed from faith to faith: as it is written, 'The just shall live by faith.'" In this passage, Paul declared salvation is for everyone; it is "to the Jew first, and also to the Greek." He also carefully connected the gospel with salvation: "The gospel," he declared, "is the power of God for salvation."

Salvation itself is a basic theme of Romans; in fact, it is a basic theme of Paul's entire work and ministry. William Barclay calls it one of the "three great foundation pillars of his thought and belief," the other two being the closely-related faith and justification.

Keep in mind that salvation in the New Testament is not just about avoiding Hell and getting to Heaven; it is holistic, affecting every aspect of our lives.

For Paul, salvation had a definite beginning; thus he could speak of people *having been* saved (Romans 8:24, 11:11). He referred to that point in time when a person responds to hearing the gospel with faith and obedience by repenting, being baptized in the name of Jesus, and receiving the baptism of the Holy Spirit (Acts 2:38). But salvation is also an ongoing process, so Paul could speak of people *being* saved (I Corinthians 1:18; 15:2). It is also a future event, so he could speak of people *going to be* saved (Romans 5:9–10; 13:11). Salvation describes all that God has done to restore humankind to a covenant relationship with Him, now and in the future. It is at the core of the message of the Old and New Testaments; it is why God was manifested in the flesh, why the Cross, and why the Resurrection. It is what God is all about in terms of His relationship with human beings. As Paul J. Achtemeier says, "the kind of history about which Paul is concerned, and with which he is dealing, is history as it illumines and displays the relationship between God and the world or, to use other terminology, between Creator and creation."

The Context of Romans 10

The context of Romans 10:13–15 is salvation, the need for it, and how it can be obtained. The passage is part of Paul's explanation for the Jewish nation's rejection of the gospel. Specifically, after describing Israel's refusal to accept the gospel, he began a series of arguments dealing with potential excuses for their rejection. In 9:6–13 he declared the problem was not because of a failure of God's Word. In 9:14–18 he insisted that Israel's rejection was not because God is unjust. In 9:19–29 Paul argued that God has the right to exercise His prerogative to offer the same salvation to Gentiles and Jews alike. Beginning at 9:30, Paul described Israel's responsibility for her failure to accept the gospel. In 9:30–10:4, he pointed out that Israel pursued righteousness through the Law and failed to find it, yet the Gentiles through faith found righteousness even when they had not pursued it. In 10:5–13, he offered Old Testament support for salvation by faith in Jesus Christ. Finally, in 10:14–21, Paul argued that Israel's failure came not because of a lack of knowledge, but due to her own stubbornness.

Four Questions

In Romans 10:12–13, Paul continued his discussion on the issue of salvation, and particularly Israel's rejection of it. In chapter 3, Paul had declared that all people need salvation: "For there is no difference: For all have sinned, and come short of the glory of God" (Romans 3:22b–23). Now he reminds the Romans that just as the need of salvation is universal, so is the availability of the gospel. He said, in effect, "The Lord is not an exclusive God, but is Lord over all mankind. He is rich in grace and mercy to all who call upon Him." He then quoted Joel 2:32: "whosoever shall call on the name of the LORD shall be delivered." This is often misunderstood to mean that Paul was saying salvation comes by a simple calling out to God. Those who believe this overlook the fact that this statement is from the same prophetic passage of Joel that Peter quoted in Acts 2 in explaining the outpouring of the Holy Spirit on the Day of Pentecost. Paul was talking about the entire process of salvation outlined by Peter in Acts 2:38.

But how do people come to call on the name of the Lord, that is, obey the gospel? What brings them to this point of faith and obedience? Paul answered this with a series of four questions:

How then shall they call on him in whom they have not believed?

How shall they believe in him of whom they have not heard?

How shall they hear without a preacher?

How shall they preach, except they be sent? (Romans 10:14–15a).

The *New Bible Commentary* summarizes these questions (and reverses the order) like this: "Messengers must be sent, the message must be preached, people must hear the message, and hearing must be met by faith." It is obvious that Paul was describing the usual steps that bring people to "call on the name of the Lord" and thus be saved. This is not speculative or theoretical; it is how people are saved. Paul's whole argument here was that the claim that Israel's rejection of the gospel can be excused because she did not know about the good news is simply bogus. He proved this by pointing out messengers *have* been sent and the message *has* been preached. This whole argument breaks down if preaching the gospel is only one of many ways people come to saving faith and obedience. In other words, if this is not the way salvation comes, then maybe Israel did not know; therefore, she could not have responded in faith and obedience, and her rejection of the gospel is excusable. Paul left no room for this interpretation, and so leaves us certain that hearing the preaching of the gospel is one of the steps leading to salvation.

The Whole Gospel Preached to the Whole World

If preaching is a vital part of the normal progression toward salvation, then it necessarily follows that preaching must be available to all who would be saved. While this may seem unlikely, Paul asserted that the fact that preaching was available to all left Israel without the excuse that they had not heard the gospel. M. B. Riddle discusses this point:

> The beautiful precision of the Greek requires us to find an intimation of the certainty of the universal gospel proclamation. In the first two questions, there is an absolute negative; in the third, χωρίς occurs, implying the probability that one will preach; in the last, we have ἐάν μή, which indicates that, however men may fail to call and hear, those who will preach will certainly be sent forth. This turn of expression seems to have escaped the notice of commentators, but it points directly toward the position the Apostle is establishing: the universality of the means provided by God for the salvation of men, whether they hear or forbear.

There are five actions taking place in this passage: sending, proclaiming, hearing, believing, and calling. The first is done by God, (and the church, in conjunction with the divine calling, see Acts 13:2–4), the second action is done by the one called (the herald or preacher), the last three by the one who would be saved. None of these things, either alone or in combination, saves. Salvation is through the death, burial, and resurrection of Jesus Christ: the gospel. But since a person must believe and obey the gospel in order to obtain salvation offered through the Cross, the calling, preaching, and hearing also have a role to play in bringing the lost to the point of saving faith.

The "calling" of men and women to preach is the action of God commissioning and sending men and women to proclaim the gospel. This is what makes preaching possible as God continues to call and use people to proclaim the good news around the world. As men and women respond to the call and follow the direction of the Holy Spirit, the gospel makes its way into every corner of the globe. This preaching accomplishes the purpose of God that all may hear.

It is the act of preaching or proclaiming, and not just the content of the message (the gospel) that is in view here. As we saw in our discussion of *kerysso*, which is used in Romans 10, there is an unbreakable link between the proclamation and that which is proclaimed. Remember Runia's comment: "wherever this event is proclaimed, it inaugurates what this event has accomplished."

So we cannot escape the conclusion that preaching plays a fundamental role in salvation. Outside the person seeking salvation, no other action by human beings (other than baptizing) is part of this process. No human righteousness, no piety, no penance plays any part. In Romans 10, Paul emphasized the importance of the role of the preacher and preaching by quoting Isaiah 52:7 and Nahum 1:15, "How beautiful are the feet of them that preach the gospel of peace, and bring glad tidings of good things!" (Romans 10:15). Warren Wiersbe points out that the context of the Nahum reference was the arrival of the good news of the fall of Israel's enemy, the Assyrians. This was a *past* event. In Isaiah, the reference is to news of a *future* event: the end time, and the coming of the Lord. "But Paul used the quotation in a present application: the messengers of the Gospel taking the Good News to Israel today. . . . The remedy for Israel's rejection is in hearing the Word of the Gospel and believing on Jesus Christ."

Hearing

Preaching is part of the process, because hearing is part of the process. For the person coming to salvation, the process starts with hearing. Paul made the connection between the proclaiming of the Word and the hearing of the listener, and the coming of faith to the heart: "So then faith cometh by hearing, and hearing by the word of God" (Romans 10:17). "Hearing" as used in Romans is not just the physical process of the mind receiving and processing sound, nor is it passive attention to what is said. R. C. Sproul explains:

> Then Paul asks in verse 18: But I ask: Did they not hear? There is a play on words here in the original language between the Greek word for hearing and the Greek word for obedience. The verb "to hear" is *akouein* which simply means "to hear." The verb "to obey" is *hupokouein*. . . . Those who really hear are the ones where the message gets through and penetrates their hearts. In fact, the word *hupokouein* is found in verse 16, where it reads that they have not all accepted the gospel—literally they have not all "obeyed" the

gospel. Although we see a frequent contrast in the Scriptures between law and gospel, here we have an indication that the gospel is to be obeyed. There is an implicit command in the gospel, a call to obedience to Jesus Christ.

In verse 16, the *New Bible Commentary* points out, Paul had "made clear that the condition in this chain that has gone unfulfilled is the responsibility of those who hear the preachers of the good news to respond in obedience and faith."

In terms of the broader application, Achtemeier insists: "Whatever else this passage may be about, it is uniquely about the great importance of hearing." The word that has just been used in verse 16 in the passive voice is used in verse 17 in the active voice. "Faith cometh by *hearing*." And this active hearing is the response to the Word of God.

Gospel preaching challenges those who hear to respond to the good news with faith and obedience, and this response brings salvation. In this way, preaching is a vital part of the salvation process. We find affirmation of this in Paul's question "How shall they hear without a preacher?" (Romans 10:14), for the answer is, without doubt, they won't hear. And without hearing there is no believing, and without believing there is no obedience, and without obedience there is no salvation.

Conclusion

As we discussed in chapter 2, preaching as understood by Paul and the rest of the first-century church, was the proclamation of the good news of salvation in Jesus Christ. This proclamation did not resort to philosophy or empty rhetoric, but by the power of the Holy Spirit demonstrated the presence of God through His Word. It was effective in bringing conviction to the hearts of those who heard it, bringing them to faith in what Jesus did on the cross, and calling them to identify with Jesus' death, burial, and resurrection by obeying Peter's instructions on the Day of Pentecost: "Repent, and be baptized every one of you in the name of Jesus Christ for the remission of sins, and ye shall receive the gift of the Holy Ghost" (Acts 2:38).

Recognizing that preaching is uniquely part of the process leading to salvation does not mean there are no other ways people might first discover the gospel. Are some first convicted and attracted through a tract or a book? Certainly. Are some saved by personal scriptural study? Yes. Do others come to God after seeing a drama, hearing a song, or witnessing a gracious act by a Christian? Absolutely. God does not shackle Himself to one way of accomplishing His will in an individual's life, much as He does not do so with the sequence of obedience and experience found in Acts 2:38. Most will repent, then be baptized, then receive the Holy Spirit; but this sequence is not the experience of everyone. While none receive the Spirit before repenting, many receive it before baptism, as did Cornelius's household in Acts 10. This does not negate the need for baptism; it just means the chronological order is not rigid. So with preaching; while a preacher preaching the Word will play an undeniable role in all being saved, preaching need not be the first—and certainly not the only—encounter with truth.

We are all like the Ethiopian eunuch. He sincerely searched the Scriptures, obviously hungry to understand them and the God they presented. So that his faith might bring him to salvation, God sent a preacher; his name was Philip. When Philip asked, "Do you understand what you are reading?" the Ethiopian replied, "How can I, except some man should guide me?" (Acts 8:30–31). Philip was invited to get in the chariot with the eunuch, and when he asked Philip to explain a passage from Isaiah 53, "Philip opened his mouth, and began at the same scripture, and preached unto him Jesus" (Acts 8:35). The proclamation of the gospel resulted in faith and obedience by the hearer: "And as they went on their way, they came unto a certain water: and the eunuch said, 'See, here is water; what doth hinder me to be baptized?' . . . And he commanded the chariot to stand still: and they went down both into the water, both Philip and the eunuch; and he baptized him" (Acts 8:36, 38).

In coming to salvation, we all need a guide. That is the job of preaching.

Sources Cited in Chapter 3

William Barclay, The Letter to the Romans (Edinburgh: The Saint Andrews Press, 1975), rev. ed.

Paul J. Achtemeier, Romans, IBCTP (Louisville: John Knox Press, 1985).

D. A. Carson, R. T. France, J. A. Motyer, and G. J. Wenham, eds. New Bible Commentary: 21st Century Edition (4th ed. Leicester, England; Downers Grove, IL: InterVarsity Press, 1994).

John Peter Lange, Philip Schaff, F. R. Fay, and M. B. Riddle; J. F. Hurst, tr. A Commentary on the Holy Scriptures: Romans (Bellingham, WA: Logos Bible Software, 2008).

Wolfgang Friedrich, "Preaching" in Gerhard Kittel, Gerhard Friedrich, eds., Geoffrey W. Bromiley tr., Theological Dictionary of the New Testament (Grand Rapids: Eerdmans, 1964–76).

Klaas Runia, "What is Preaching According to the New Testament?" The Tyndale Biblical Theology Lecture for 1976, delivered at the School of Oriental and African Studies, London, on January 4th, 1977.

Warren W. Wiersbe, The Bible Exposition Commentary (Wheaton, IL: Victor Books, 1996).

R. C. Sproul, The Gospel of God: An Exposition of Romans (Great Britain: Christian Focus Publications, 1994).

Part Two

The Preacher

> The orator persuades by moral character when his speech is delivered in such a manner as to render him worthy of confidence; for we feel confidence in a greater degree and more readily in persons of worth in regard to everything in general.
>
> Aristotle

Now that we have defined preaching and discussed the biblical basis for it, let's look at the process of preaching, that is, how is it done? What are its components, and maybe most importantly, how can we learn to do it and do it effectively?

Can preaching be learned? It is a spiritual event; that is sure. It is a collaboration between God and humans, so why do we need to learn how to do it? Can't we just leave it up to God? Didn't God tell one of His prophets not to worry about what he would say, that God would fill his mouth with words? Yes, He did say that. When Jeremiah was struggling with the call of God upon his life, one of his arguments was that he could not preach, he was only a young man, he had nothing to say! God's answer went to the heart of what was really bothering Jeremiah: rejection. It wasn't lack of ability or knowledge that lay at the root of Jeremiah's reluctance; it was fear. "Be not afraid of their faces: for I am with thee to deliver thee, saith the LORD. Then the LORD put forth his hand, and touched my mouth. And the LORD said unto me, Behold, I have put my words in thy mouth" (Jeremiah 1:8–9). It was a reassuring vision for a scared young man, overwhelmed by the immensity and difficulty of the call to preach. This was not God describing the method for preaching for all time; He was simply assuring Jeremiah that with God's help he would be able to do what he was called to do.

While preaching is spiritual and demands the anointing of God, as we saw in chapter 1, it is also communication. It is public speaking. There are fundamentals to effective public speaking that can and must be learned. They are essential to success. They may seem simple or unimportant, but failing to master them will cripple your preaching from the beginning.

Albert Einstein had to learn his numbers, then addition and subtraction. After that, he had to memorize the multiplication tables and learn long division. Then came geometry, algebra, trigonometry, and calculus. Step by step he had to master these fundamentals before he had the skill to arrive at $E=MC^2$. Powerful preaching has many components. Many of them are spiritual and wholly dependent on the Spirit of God; others are down-to-earth. Coupled with the Spirit, these are fundamentals of communication. Learn them from the basic to the advanced, and God will put His words in your mouth.

Often in discussions of preaching, the process of preaching is said to have three components. These three components are present in every sermon preached, regardless of the type of sermon. They are:

1. The Preacher
2. The Preparation
3. The Presentation

As you see, these have nothing to do with the number of points used, or memorable alliteration, or the proper use of illustrations. These three are more fundamental than that; they are the foundation of every sermon. It is not an oversimplification to say that if these are right, the sermon will be right, but if these three are not right, nothing can make the final product right.

This description of preaching is not new. In fact, it is based on Aristotle's description of effective public speaking: "Now the proofs furnished by the speech are of three kinds. The first depends upon the moral character of the speaker, the second upon putting the hearer into a certain frame of mind, the third upon the speech itself, in so far as it proves or seems to prove." Aristotle lists them in a different order (his order is the preacher, the presentation, and the preparation), but you get the point. These three ingredients will serve as a rough outline for the remainder of this book. We will study each of these ingredients in turn, beginning with the preacher.

4

THE CALL TO PREACH

> I determined early in my ministry that I could not afford to be good at golf. I decided to be good at preaching. You have to choose what you will be good at, because you can be good at only a very few things.
>
> Quoted without attribution in *12 Essential Skills for Great Preaching* by Wayne McDill

> And He appointed twelve that they might be with Him, and that He might send them forth to preach. This is the beginning of the preacher's training, and the essential part of it—to be WITH HIM and to be SENT FORTH BY HIM.
>
> Arthur E. Gregory

At the heart of every sermon is the preacher who is preaching it. A person's own relationship with God, with the Word, and with the surrounding world will color and affect everything that is said. It is possible to preach, and not be a real man or woman of God. It is possible to be eloquent, and even affect those who hear you. But it is impossible, in the long term, to keep your true self from being revealed.

To be a preacher but not have a real and deep relationship with God is to rob your efforts of true persuasive power. Your results will be only those results that a well-crafted and eloquent piece of public speaking can bring. We must not confuse the power of effective speaking with the power of God. There have always been powerful speakers who brought great crowds, indeed whole nations, to follow them, for good or ill. You must be much more than that. You need the anointing of God and the power of the Word in order to have an eternal effect on those who hear you. Without those two things, your preaching will become tinkling brass and sounding cymbals.

If you do not intend to dedicate yourself to a daily, lifelong commitment to developing and maintaining a genuine walk with God, then do something else; for the sake of those who hear you, and for your own sake, don't be a preacher. Preaching the Word of God is not a profession, it is not a job, nor is it a career. It is a high and holy calling, a sacred commission from God Himself. To approach it lightly, to seek it for the chance to be in front of a crowd merely to seek attention or applause is a foolish and even dangerous thing to do.

Called by God

The beginning of every true ministry is the call of God. Of this call, William Sangster wrote:

> Called to preach! Commissioned of God to teach the word! A herald of the great King! A witness of the Eternal Gospel! Could any work be more high and holy? To this supreme task God sent His only begotten Son. In all the frustration and confusion of the times, is it possible to imagine a work comparable in importance with that of proclaiming the will of God to wayward men? Not by accident, nor yet by the thrustful egotism of men, was the pulpit given central place . . . it is there of design and devotion. It is there by the logic of things. It is there as the throne of the Word of God.

It is absolutely vital to remember that God does the calling. We do not choose to be a preacher like we would choose to be, say, a lawyer, a doctor, or a salesman. God does the choosing. Our only choice is to obey or not to obey. This is never a simple, nor an easy choice. Something within us seems to recognize the far-reaching ramifications of such a choice, and it is natural to hesitate, to question, to doubt.

The call to preach is not simply the plan of God for our lives, nor is it just the will of God for our lives. God does have a will and a plan for the lives of all His children, no doubt about that. Sometimes we talk of someone being called to do something other than preach; this is true, because there are certainly lesser callings: doctor, lawyer, president, or king. *But this is the call to preach.* This call touches not only time, and life here, but this touches eternal life, because preaching is integral to the process of salvation, as we have seen in chapter 3: "How then shall they call on him in whom they have not believed? And how shall they believe in him of whom they have not heard? And how shall they hear without a preacher? And how shall they preach, except they be sent?" (Romans 19:14–15a). This call is how God sends those who preach, and only those who have this call can truly preach.

God's call is forever. Look at Romans 11:29: "For the gifts and calling of God are without repentance." God does not rescind His call, even though we may refuse it, abuse it, or even disqualify ourselves from following it. To simply ignore it and live our lives fulfilling our own ambitions and plans is a dangerous business. "And Jesus said unto him, No man, having put his hand to the plow, and looking back, is fit for the kingdom of God" (Luke 9:62). The context here is the call to preach the gospel.

Be Sure, Then Go Ahead

Because the decision to acknowledge and obey the call to preach is a serious, life-altering choice, we must approach it with the gravity it demands. After Jesus, the greatest preacher of all time was Paul. His ministry has affected the world as no other, yet even he sometimes marveled that such a responsibility as preaching the only saving gospel was placed on the shoulders of human beings. "For we are unto God a sweet savour of Christ, in them that are saved, and in them that perish: To the one we are the savour of death unto death; and to the other the savour of life unto life. And who is sufficient for these things?" (II Corinthians 2:15–16). To engage in preaching because you love the attention or want to impress somebody is to court disaster. You preach because you have no choice.

There is a cost to being a preacher, and not everyone is equipped to handle that cost. James may have had this in mind when he wrote, "My brethren, be not many masters, knowing that we shall receive the greater condemnation" (James 3:1). The word rendered "masters" could be better translated *instructors* so that the meaning of James's comment becomes "Many should not be instructors, knowing the weight that they must bear." All this goes to your motive for wanting to be a preacher. For the vast majority of preachers, there is little recognition, even less applause. Most labor their lives away in obscurity, faithfully fulfilling their call. Most will not be rich, famous, or by the world's reckoning, even successful. But they will fulfill what God called them to do. They will pluck many from the burning, and great will be their reward, not here, but in Heaven. If you want anything other than a life of service, self-denial, and commitment to an eternal cause more and more out of step with modern times, don't be a preacher.

My pastor A. E. Carney used to advise those who came to him saying they felt a call to preach: "If you can do anything else, don't preach." I have on occasion shared that advice, and it has sometimes been misunderstood; a few times it has even offended someone. Once, after a class where I quoted Brother Carney, I was approached by a young lady who was upset. She said, "Brother Jones, it is wrong to say that only those who are not able to do anything else should preach! If we teach that, we will prevent our best, most able young people from being preachers, and those are the ones we need!" Of course she was right, but she missed the point. (I should have communicated it better!) When Brother Carney said, "If you can do anything else, don't preach," he didn't mean preachers should be drawn from those who are so inept and unqualified they can't make a living any other way. He meant that no matter what other fields of labor call to you, no matter how able and talented you may be for something else, no matter how much you may desire to do something else, if you are truly called to preach, you will have no other choice, you simply *must* be a preacher. So, if you find in spite of feeling like you are called to preach, you can be happy, fulfilled, and satisfied doing something else, then you weren't truly called to preach. If you are called, there is just no other choice: "For though I preach the gospel, I have nothing to glory of: for necessity is laid upon me; yea, woe is unto me, if I preach not the gospel!" (I Corinthians 9:16).

If there are reservations, do something else until you know for sure. Once you know, commit yourself totally. Never ask God for an escape clause: "If this doesn't work out, I can always . . . ." To enter the ministry with plans for exiting doesn't work. It doesn't work for a marriage; it won't work for a ministry. You will get discouraged, you will feel like quitting, but if you are truly called, and completely committed, you will make it through, simply because there is no choice.

Response to the Call

It is important to realize the call is just that—a call. It doesn't make you a man or woman of God. It is what you do with that call that makes you a man or woman of God. The call is the starting point, the foundation. It must be built upon.

So how should you respond to the call? Simply put, get busy. Involve yourself in the life of a local church. One of the qualifications for a preacher we will explore in the next chapter is "not a novice." A novice is a beginner, one who lacks experience. Experience comes only with time and involvement. You need experience—not at preaching—at living, at praying, at witnessing.

Almost forty years ago, Brother Fred Foster was teaching a class for young ministers during a district meeting in Louisiana. During the lesson, he made a statement that I wrote on the flyleaf of my brand-new Thompson Chain-Reference Bible. It reads: "You can be young in years but old in hours, if you haven't lost any time." Don't expect pulpit time right away, but don't sit and sulk; get busy. Start pouring yourself into Bible study, sermon study, ministry study. Go to your pastor and put yourself at his service, then do what he asks, no matter how menial. I started out mowing the church yard. Jeff Arnold cleaned the bathrooms. Almost every preacher who is in ministry today started out just like us. Meditate on Matthew 25:21. "His lord said unto him, Well done, thou good and faithful servant: thou hast been faithful over a few things, I will make thee ruler over many things: enter thou into the joy of thy lord."

Make a place for your calling. I have met preachers who are bitter at what they consider the unfairness of their ministerial organization. You have to know somebody, or be kin to somebody to have a chance they say. I don't claim human organizations are not prey to some of the same ills that plague any group of human beings, but there are too many examples of men and women of no connection or birth who have had great ministries and tremendous impact for that excuse to hold water. You are responsible to make your calling and election sure. I received a letter from one preacher who surrendered his preaching credentials from the United Pentecostal Church International because, as he angrily pointed out, "I have been licensed two years and the UPC still hasn't found me a church to pastor!" Phillips Brooks says such people "are of the kind who make no place in life for themselves, but wait till someone kindly makes one for them and drops them into it."

It should not be easy to be a man or woman of God. It ought to cost as much in terms of sacrifice, commitment, and effort as to be a doctor or lawyer, and maybe even more. If you are blessed to have a leg up, someone who can help you on the way, thank God for it; but if not, make your way. God called you; your job is to obey the calling regardless of how hard the road.

When I began preaching, I knew virtually no one, and no one knew me. My father was not a preacher. Neither of my grandfathers served the Lord. I did have the advantage of a great pastor, A. E. Carney, who made calls and encouraged his friends to give me an opportunity to preach, and a few of them did. Mostly though, like so many others who started out the same time I did (Carlton Coon, Tommy Parker, Tim Mahoney, Mark Christian, Ronnie LaCombe, Murrell Cornwell, Darrel Johns, and many, many others), I had to carve out a place for myself. There were lots of weeks with nowhere to preach. Often during Christmas, when there were hardly any revivals, I took odd jobs. Sometimes I was able to help with the yearly inventory at the car dealership where my dad was parts manager.

I learned to preach conducting revivals in small churches in small communities: Six-Mile, Doodle Fork, Jigger, Red Star, Oberlin. The crowds were small, but they were forgiving of a novice trying to learn how to preach effectively. It was akin to learning to swim by jumping in and hoping for the best. I hauled my little library around with me, structured my days around devotion and study, and put together sermons. Some of them were pretty good. Many more of them were bad. I worked on sentences, how to say things effectively and memorably. I thought about how to gauge the impact of each point and how to order them for maximum effect. Without realizing it, I learned about cadence, rhythm, the power of illustration, and how to tell a story. I learned this by experience. I preached, often eight times a week, night after night.

And I learned from other preachers. As I watched them, I began to analyze their preaching and look for what worked and why. There is no richer source for learning to preach than the effective preachers around you. However, a word of caution: in learning from them, avoid the trap of impersonating. It is a mistake to adopt a pulpit personality not your own. Of course you will use syntax and sentence structure in the pulpit that is different from everyday speech. But to simply imitate another preacher is distracting to the congregation at best, and amusing at worst. It can even be a little weird. Moreover, it robs the church of something we need: your voice.

Make a place for yourself by serving and doing what is at hand with an unwavering commitment to doing your best. The calling will make a way; your ministry will be born. Learn to talk, to walk, then run. Opportunities will come if you will be faithful. You cannot see very far down the road. None of us can. But you can start today, right where you are, doing what you have a chance to do. The journey is long and it can be hard, but take it from one who has been on it for more than forty-five years: it is worth it. Answer the call and start today.

Sources Cited in Chapter 4

William Sangster, *The Approach to Preaching* (London: Epworth Press, 1951. Repr., Grand Rapids: Baker, 1974).

Phillips Brooks, *Lectures On Preaching Delivered Before the Divinity School of Yale College in January and February, 1877* (New York: E. P. Dutton, 1878).

5

THE PREACHER'S QUALIFICATIONS

A master is somebody who, every single day tries to pursue perfection. There's a lot of days you would rather take the shortcut than to do it as well as it can be done, and better than the day before. A master is somebody who has the work ethic, who has the discipline, who has the passion to do what they do incrementally better each day until the day they die.

Ryan Neil

You can be young in years but old in hours, if you haven't lost any time.

Fred Foster

As in any other endeavor, there are qualifications to be a preacher. They have nothing to do with your last name, your parents' occupations, the size of your home church, or your pastor's reputation. They also have nothing to do with education, experience, skills, or any of the other accomplishments that fill résumés. They all have to do with you: your choices in life, your character, how you spend your time, who you hang out with. All these play a part in whether you are qualified to preach or not.

Just as it tells us what preaching is, the Bible tells us what a preacher is. In writing to a young preacher, Timothy, Paul gave a list of the qualifications necessary to be a preacher. Although he was primarily describing a pastor, his list fits all preachers regardless of their ministry position.

> This is a true saying, If a man desire the office of a bishop, he desireth a good work. A bishop then must be blameless, the husband of one wife, vigilant, sober, of good behaviour, given to hospitality, apt to teach; not given to wine, no striker, not greedy of filthy lucre; but patient, not a brawler, not covetous; one that ruleth well his own house, having his children in subjection with all gravity (For if a man know not how to rule his own house, how shall he take care of the church of God?), not a novice, lest being lifted up with pride he fall into the condemnation of the devil. Moreover he must have a good report of them which are without; lest he fall into reproach and the snare of the devil (I Timothy 3:1–7).

In his letter to Titus, Paul gave a list of qualifications for those who would be ordained as elders in the churches in Crete:

> For this cause left I thee in Crete, that thou shouldest set in order the things that are wanting, and ordain elders in every city, as I had appointed thee: If any be blameless, the husband of one wife, having faithful children not accused of riot or unruly. For a bishop must be blameless, as the steward of God; not selfwilled, not soon angry, not given to wine, no striker, not given to filthy lucre; But a lover of hospitality, a lover of good men, sober, just, holy, temperate, Holding fast the faithful word as he hath been taught, that he may be able by sound doctrine both to exhort and to convince the gainsayers (Titus 1:5).

You should carefully study and deeply consider these qualifications. There are many in these two passages to choose from, but we will focus on seven of them: discipline, moderation, honesty, good stewardship (of both money and time), sincerity, morality, and faithfulness. Let's briefly look at each of them in turn.

Discipline

This is the most important because all the others rest on this one. Simply stated, someone who has no discipline will have none of the other traits either because they are all extensions of discipline. None of them can exist without it. For preachers especially, discipline is vital because we don't punch a time clock, have a supervisor to oversee our activities, or account to anyone for how our time is spent. Self-discipline is crucial.

Moderation

Closely related to discipline is moderation. Paul probably had moderation in mind when he wrote I Corinthians 6:12. "All things are lawful unto me, but all things are not expedient: all things are lawful for me, but I will not be brought under the power of any." The context is the power of sin, but the larger view is "meats for the belly, and the belly for meats" (6:13). In other words, power to dominate us doesn't always come from things that are sinful or addictive in themselves, but from us allowing them to consume our lives. Hobbies, sports, social media, and all the interests that consume our time and fill our thoughts must be tightly controlled and kept in their place, or they will spiral out of control. Moderation in all earthly things is a worthy creed.

Honesty

"Resolve to be honest at all events; and if in your judgment you cannot be an honest lawyer, resolve to be honest without being a lawyer." So advised lawyer Abraham Lincoln. It almost seems absurd to remind ministers they should be honest, but the Bible does just that. Dishonesty is a habit of mind and attitude. If you exaggerate, mislead, or deal falsely with people, not only will you face God in the end, you will, in this life without fail, lose the respect of people. Your reputation is vital to your success as a minister. Without fundamental honesty, you will be without a ministry.

Stewardship

A steward is one who manages the possessions of others. Our wealth, our time, and our talents do not belong to us; they belong to God. He allows us to use them. How we use these assets for Him determines whether we are good or bad stewards. In our management of time, money, and abilities we must put to work the three attributes we just talked about: discipline, moderation, and honesty. The lack of any of these three shows itself most often in the management of money. Unpaid bills, living beyond one's means, and financial dishonesty all reveal a chaotic inner life. Anyone can run into hard times, but handling them with discipline and honesty not only builds a good reputation, it builds the inner person.

Sincerity

Simply put, sincerity is living what you preach. It is being real. By its nature sincerity is not something you can try to be, or act out. You can force yourself into a disciplined lifestyle, develop good habits, and become a person of integrity, but sincerity doesn't work like that. I don't mean you cannot commit to being sincere and monitor your behavior to insure you mean what you say and only be what you are; I mean if you are insincere, you will act like you have integrity, discipline, and honesty, but really you won't. You will say all the right things and instruct those who hear you in all the biblical teachings on righteousness, but you will give your secret self a pass and justify a lifestyle that is not what you teach others. While discipline is the exercise of will to be what we should be, sincerity is the spiritual engine behind the acts of discipline. Sincerity is not an act of will; it is an act of relationship. To know Jesus and to sincerely be like Him must be the heart's desire of all of us.

Morality

Like so many of these traits, it seems strange to point out to preachers that they should be moral. Why would anyone even imagine that a person could be a preacher without being moral? Yet, examples are plentiful of preachers failing in this fundamental area. Your relationships with the opposite sex must be guarded at all times. The promiscuity of our times, the laxity of social media, and the secret opportunities of the Internet, all demand a commitment to morality; not because you want to be a preacher, but because you want to be right, and to be righteous.

Faithfulness

Notice Paul's final statement in his description of the qualifications for preaching that he gave to Titus: "Holding fast the faithful word as he hath been taught, that he may be able by sound doctrine both to exhort and to convince the gainsayers" (Titus 1:5). This is *why* we develop these traits in our lives. Internalize the Word. Your faithfulness to the Word will be, sooner or later, questioned by some cool preacher who has forward-sounding ideas. This preacher will attack the people who you have trusted, the church you have been part of, and even the Word itself. Holding fast doesn't imply a loose, easy grip; it pictures a death grip that, though someone is pulling with all their might to tear it away, won't let it go. Hold fast the Word, it is not only the basis of what we believe and what we do, but it defines who we are. Don't give that up without the fight of your life. To paraphrase a bumper sticker, you can have my faith in the Word when you pry it out of my cold, dead hands.

Why We Live This Way

We live by this code so that we may be effective preachers of the Word. These qualifications are not so that we will be credentialed by an organization, or honored as a minister, or even blessed by God; they are so that we will be able to effectively handle the Word of God.

This is no light matter. In II Corinthians 2, Paul discussed the awesome role of the preacher in handling the Word of God:

> Now thanks be unto God, which always causeth us to triumph in Christ, and maketh manifest the savour of his knowledge by us in every place. For we are unto God a sweet savour of Christ, in them that are saved, and in them that perish: To the one we are the savour of death unto death; and to the other the savour of life unto life. And who is sufficient for these things? For we are not as many, which corrupt the word of God: but as of sincerity, but as of God, in the sight of God speak we in Christ (II Corinthians 2:14–17).

Even a cursory examination of this passage reveals some sobering truths about the relationship between preachers' inner lives and their preaching. First, we are used of God; what we do is ultimately not the result of talent, skill, or education. In the end, preaching is a divine thing, a God thing. When we preach, God is using us to manifest the savour (reveal the influence) of the knowledge of God.

Second, Paul insisted that the Word changes people, for good or ill when it is revealed through anointed preaching. If people accept and obey, it brings life to them; if they reject it, it brings death. But either way, they are changed forever by the influence of the preached Word. These are souls, and these souls will live eternally in Heaven or Hell, in large part because they have been persuaded or not persuaded by our preaching. Of course they are exercising their own free will, but Paul refused to exonerate us; rather, he emphasized the role we play, when we preach the Word of God, in settling the eternal destinies of those who hear us: "And who is sufficient for these things?" (II Corinthians 2:16).

We can have no doubt that he had preaching in mind because he focuses our attention with these words: "For we are not as many which corrupt the word of God." And finally, he explained the only way any human being could possibly bear such responsibility: "but as of sincerity, . . . as of God, in the sight of God speak we in Christ" (II Corinthians 2:17).

Indeed, who is worthy to handle such a powerful thing as the Word of God, which is life or death to those that hear it? Only sincere men or women, only those who recognize fully their own frailty as human beings, but cannot escape the fact that they have been called. They know they cannot be worthy; they can only be obedient.

How can we develop the sort of life that equips us to deal with the eternal issues of God's Word? The sincere life must begin with the right convictions. Convictions are our unshakable core beliefs. Core beliefs are nonnegotiable doctrines and values that we believe in and hold. Regardless of changes in culture, public mores, or legal standards, our core values do not change. Our identity as the church as well as our individual relationships with God are reflected in our core values and beliefs. Without such unshakable convictions, we cannot hope to properly handle the Word of God. In his book, *The Apostolic Church in the Twenty-First Century*, David K. Bernard identifies three categories of core values: apostolic identity, apostolic unity, and apostolic revival. Within these categories are the basic beliefs that form the foundation of our Christianity. Here is how Brother Bernard describes them:

> As apostolic believers we model ourselves after the New Testament church. These three core values are prominent in Acts 2, which describes the beginning of the church, the message of the twelve apostles, and the life of the early believers. In this account, we see a strong commitment to doctrinal identity (verse 42), including the deity of Jesus (verses 21, 36), the plan of salvation (verses 4, 38), and separation from the world (verse 40). We also see a strong example of unity—in fellowship, prayer, sacrificial giving,

and worship (verses 43–47). Finally, we see true revival, with wonders, signs, discipleship, and numerical growth (verses 43, 47).

Your dedication to these core beliefs of identity, unity, and revival shape your inner person to reflect Jesus Christ. As you personally become more and more like Him, your preaching takes on an aspect impossible to produce any other way. You truly become His messenger. People hear His voice when you preach.

John R. W. Stott, in *Between Two Worlds*, discusses the convictions that are necessary to form the foundation of the preacher's ministry. Let's look at Stott's list:

The first is our conviction about God.
- God is light. As the nature of light is to shine it is God's nature to reveal Himself.
- God has acted, both in creation and in redemption.
- God has spoken. Not only in deeds has He revealed himself, He has actually spoken.

The second is our conviction about the Word.
- The Scripture is God's Word written. As such it is the basis of all we say.
- God still speaks through His Word. It is not a dead textbook of the past.
- God's Word is powerful. Do you expect something to happen every time you preach?

The Preacher's Qualifications

Third, we need a conviction about the church.
- It is a creation of God's Word. As such, it is dependent on the Word.

Along with that we need a conviction about pastoring.
- God still gives overseers to His church, and always will.

Finally, we need a conviction about preaching.
- The preacher should preach the Word. Not opinion, not politics, but the Word.

These convictions form the bedrock of our attitude toward what we are called to do. We should pay particular attention to the second one. We must never lose our absolute confidence in the Bible as God's Word. It is not just a source of stories and texts that illustrate successful principles that, if followed, enrich and bring purpose to our lives; it is the source of power that enables us to live by those principles. Preaching the Word of God does not just save its hearers, it transforms them. Once we come to be absolutely convinced of this truth, the final conviction is formed: the preacher must preach the Word.

I am saddened when I see preachers using the pulpit to educate, inform, even inspire, but do so without the Bible as the source and center of the sermon. While the principles they are communicating may be valuable or even essential, to base them on psychology, human experience, or business principles is to strip them of the power that the Word brings. In the next chapter, we will look at the fundamental requirement of all preachers: preach the Word.

Sources Cited in Chapter 5

David K. Bernard, *The Apostolic Church in the Twenty-First Century* (Hazelwood, MO: Word Aflame Press, 2014).

John R. W. Stott, *Between Two Worlds* (Grand Rapids: Eerdmans, 1982).

6

PREACH THE WORD

Three words should be clearly understood and kept distinct in our thoughts: gift, knowledge, and ability. Gift, or talent, comes from God. Knowledge stems from prayerful, concentrated and conscientious study of the Word of God. Ability is developed as the gift is exercised in an atmosphere of spirituality.

Alfred P. Gibbs

Sermon delivery derives its reason for existence from its relationship to sermon content. That relationship may be specified as one that *maximizes the message and minimizes the messenger.*

Al Fasol

The so-called *emergent* philosophy we hear of today, among other dreadful failings, robs the pulpit of its authority and the preacher of his or her dignity. This philosophy is nothing new. There has always been this insidious falsehood that the preacher knows no more, has no more insight, no more understanding of God and His Word than the newest convert in the pew. "I know no more than you, so come, we will search together. Your opinions and your comments are as important as mine." So preaching is abandoned for dialogue, and absolute truth for relativistic foolishness. "Men have always passed by" such nonsense, said Phillips Brooks 135 years ago, and they always will.

This is exactly what Paul had in mind when he insisted to the young preacher, Timothy: "Study to show thyself approved, a workman which needeth not be ashamed" (II Timothy 2:15). Your calling expresses God's confidence in you; what you do with His calling determines your effectiveness and success as a preacher.

No one in his right mind would put his health and life in the hands of a doctor who proclaimed, "I know no more about medicine than you. Come on in and we will discuss your problems, and with your knowledge and mine together we can perhaps find a solution that you can believe in." I want a second opinion! Neither would anyone seek legal advice from someone who had no more training and experience in the law than she had. We wouldn't even trust our car to a mechanic who was no more knowledgeable about automobiles than we were. Why should people trust their souls to a preacher who claims to be no more knowledgeable about the things of God than they?

Our authority is found not in the fact that we preach, but in the content of our preaching. Silly, shallow, entertainment-oriented preaching is no more worthy of attention than any other effort at public speaking, but a sermon that contains the truths of the eternal Word commands a response.

The early church was consumed with a desire to take the gospel to the world. Even before their eyes were opened to the fact that Christianity would not be just another sect of Judaism, they spread the news of the gospel everywhere they went. Just as Jesus said they should, they began at Jerusalem. After the Day of Pentecost, revival spread across the city, great miracles drew crowds including those who lived in surrounding towns, and thousands were filled with the Holy Ghost and baptized in Jesus' name. What was striking in the account of the Jerusalem revival was how powerless the council's members were to stop the revival and how utterly terrified they were of uneducated and unsophisticated men. The disciples were arrested, threatened, released, rearrested, delivered from prison in the middle of the night, then arrested again, only to be released again. The council was paralyzed by fear. It is also amazing to realize that the council was not afraid of the miracles the disciples worked, or the huge crowds that came to hear them preach. It was the preaching itself that they feared. Over and over the council commanded the disciples to stop the preaching and teaching: "And they called them, and commanded them not to speak at all nor teach in the name of Jesus" (Acts 4:18).

Their threats did not stop the disciples; they continued to spread the good news everywhere. The results of their fearless and faithful preaching were incredible: people were filled with the Holy Ghost and baptized every day. It may be that in a matter of weeks as many as fifty thousand were saved. What was the secret of this great revival? It was not buildings, organized effort, or structure. Their secret was simple: the frustrated council itself described it best in Acts 5:28. "Did not we straitly command you that ye should not teach in this name? and, behold, ye have filled Jerusalem with your doctrine, and intend to bring this man's blood upon us."

The success of the disciples was not based on personality, talent, or people skills. It was their preaching and teaching of doctrine, pure and simple. The church in Jerusalem just would not quit proclaiming the doctrine, and God gave them revival.

"Ye have filled Jerusalem with your doctrine." The truth of the doctrine is the engine of revival; it is the hope of the world. Doctrine defines the church; it is what we preach, but it is much more: it is what we are. It is what makes us distinctive. To abandon doctrine is to abandon our very identity. In spite of what those who hate truth may say, doctrine, properly preached and taught, does not divide; it gathers people together, it turns their faces toward God. There is a powerful attraction embedded in truth that calls to men and women in every culture and in every time.

Not so long ago I heard a preacher preaching from Hebrews 6. That happens to be a chapter that has long fascinated me, so I gave him all my attention. I was shocked and saddened by his comments on this wonderful passage. Here's what the Word of God says:

> Therefore leaving the principles of the doctrine of Christ, let us go on unto perfection; not laying again the foundation of repentance from dead works, and of faith toward God, Of the doctrine of baptisms, and of laying on of hands, and of resurrection of the dead, and of eternal judgment. And this will we do, if God permit (Hebrews 6:1–3).

The preacher focused on these first three verses of the chapter, and more especially the first verse. He taught that the Word was urging us to leave behind our immature fixation on doctrine. It served us well in the past when we were small, weak, and needed protection from the enemies' wiles that would have destroyed us. But now we are grown up; we don't need to be so hard-nosed now. All doctrine does at this point is to separate us from others that we could learn from and who could learn from us. So, as the writer of Hebrews says, let us leave the principles of the doctrine behind us, and go on into perfection.

What the preacher did, of course, was to pick and choose the parts of the passage that fit his argument and ignore the rest. If we only read verse 1 up to the semicolon and stop there, the argument that the preacher made that night sounds true. But the words that follow the semicolon modify the words that precede it. To ignore the words in the second half of the verse is to miss the meaning of the words in the first half.

Look carefully at the words after the semicolon: "not laying *again* the foundation." Now we see clearly the meaning of the word "leaving." It does not suggest abandoning the doctrine, but building upon it. No building can ever be built if the foundation is constantly being torn up and re-constructed. The writer is telling us to stop re-laying the foundation, but to settle it once and for all; then, finish the structure on that foundation.

It has been said that it is better to debate the issue without settling it, than to settle it without debating it. This may be true, but to constantly debate without finally settling the issue is surely the worst result of all. Especially when it occurs within our own hearts, it is evident that constant debate is paralyzing. Hebrews 6 issues a clear call to end the debate. Certainly it is a scriptural concept to put ourselves in remembrance of our faith. But there must be some foundational truths that are inviolate. Some things must finally and for all time be settled. These are the anchor of our souls; they are the foundation upon which all other faith rests.

As a builder pours and finishes the foundation, and then completes the building, we must pour and finish the foundation of our faith. Hebrews 6 is not a call to move from doctrine, it is a call to establish it. Not laying again the foundation is the imagery not of abandonment, but of settling with certainty, then building up from there. Foundations are not made to be abandoned; they are made to be built upon.

This matters because the most vital part of any building is the foundation. The importance of the foundation cannot be exaggerated, since the foundation provides stability for the entire structure. The Word of God uses this imagery to teach us that our lives must have a foundation strong enough to withstand the storms of life and to provide the basis of building a greater structure to the glory of God.

What happens when there is no good foundation? Often the building collapses. This is what Jesus described in Matthew 7:24–27:

> Therefore whosoever heareth these sayings of mine, and doeth them, I will liken him unto a wise man, which built his house upon a rock: And the rain descended, and the floods came, and the winds blew, and beat upon that house; and it fell not: for it was founded upon a rock. And every one that heareth these sayings of mine, and doeth them not, shall be likened unto a foolish man, which built his house upon the sand: And the rain descended, and the floods came, and the winds blew, and beat upon that house; and it fell: and great was the fall of it.

The foundation was so poor that the building collapsed, and all the labor of constructing it was wasted. We have all seen those who seemed to be doing well, appeared to be strong in the Lord; yet they suddenly collapsed in a time of stress, almost overnight. Their dramatic demise took our breath away, and made us wonder how such things can happen. The truth is they simply had no solid foundation; they had never really settled their core beliefs. All they had done is gone along with the way they were brought up or had been taught when they first came to the Lord. They had never laid the foundation solid and firm in their own hearts. When our core beliefs are always up for grabs, our entire lives rest on a shaky foundation.

Sometimes the collapse is not so swift or dramatic, but a slow weakening until one day the structure is beyond repair. Usually this means the foundation is weak because it does not rest on Bible truth, or perhaps it is diluted by human opinion or the demands of the present culture. Michael Pollan in *A Place of My Own* describes the danger of a foundation that is not solid and true:

> But long before our house would collapse, the shifting of its foundation would set in motion an incremental process that would doom the building just as surely. The slightest movement of the footings would ramify throughout the structure, gradually eroding one after another of its right angles; "trueness," in the carpenter's sense, is the first casualty of a poor foundation. First the door frame falls out of square, since it is braced on only three sides. Then the windows. A building is a brittle thing, and eventually its seal against the weather will be broken-through a crack in the roof, perhaps, or in the slight discrepancy that arises between a ninety-degree window sash and what has become an eighty-nine-degree window frame. Now a drip at a time, water enters the building

and the process of its decomposition begins. As Joe put it, "Pretty soon, it's termite food."

What then should be our foundation? The basis of an enduring foundation is found in Ephesians 2:20: "And are built upon the foundation of the apostles and prophets, Jesus Christ himself being the chief corner stone." The most interesting aspect of this analogy is that Jesus is not the foundation; He is the chief cornerstone. The cornerstone is not part of the foundation, but the whole structure rests on it.

Let me hurry to say that, of course, in one sense, Jesus is our foundation: "According to the grace of God which is given unto me, as a wise masterbuilder, I have laid the foundation, and another buildeth thereon. But let every man take heed how he buildeth thereupon. For other foundation can no man lay than that is laid, which is Jesus Christ" (I Corinthians 3:10–11).

But something else is in view in Ephesians 2. Among other things, Jesus is shown as the cornerstone because the emphasis is deliberately being placed on the apostles and prophets. This is to focus on the truth that our foundation is the Word of God, which God wrote through the apostles and prophets. The reason Paul was inspired to describe the foundation as being the written Word instead of being Jesus Himself was because he wanted us to escape the trap the Jews fell into. The Jews did not recognize Jesus because they were looking for a Messiah that was the product of their own imaginations instead of the Word. You cannot build your life successfully on an imaginary Jesus. Our foundation is the Jesus of the Scriptures. A lot of people are in love with an idea, but not the reality. The message is that your house must be built on the Word. That will determine whether it stands or falls.

The foundation for our Christian life is our "most holy faith" (Jude 20), which is the same as "the faith which was once delivered unto the saints" (Jude 3). Doctrine is not just our introduction to God, it is the basis of our continuing relationship with Him. We cannot know Him outside His revelation of Himself, and that revelation is embodied in doctrine. That means to abandon doctrine is to abandon knowing Him. The church of the Book of Acts learned this truth very early: "And they continued steadfastly in the apostles' doctrine and fellowship, and in breaking of bread, and in prayers" (Acts 2:42).

Doctrine is powerful as the engine of real revival and essential as the foundation of life for a simple reason: it *is* the truth. There is a power truth has just because it is the truth. Truth has a life of its own. Here are some characteristics of the truth that are important for us to keep at the forefront of our thinking.

First, the truth is absolute. That means regardless of time, situation, or circumstance, the truth is the truth. It needs no one to agree with it to be true. It needs no one to believe in it to be true. This is astonishing to us who live in a society governed by polling data. If we read that 64 percent of Americans believe something, our subconscious reaction is to believe that makes it true. But 64 percent can be wrong. What percentage of people once believed the world was flat? What percentage once believed man would never fly? Indeed, the truth is, 100 percent of people can be wrong: "For what if some did not believe? shall their unbelief make the faith of God without effect? God forbid: yea, let God be true, but every man a liar" (Romans 3:3–4a).

The rejection of the concept of absolute truth has corrupted other fundamental aspects of logical thinking. One example is the change in the definition of the word tolerance. Tolerance means: "To recognize and respect the rights, beliefs, or practices of others." It does *not* mean one has to approve, or declare as right, the beliefs or practices of others. If a preacher tells people they are saved without the Holy Ghost or without being baptized in Jesus' name, I respect his right to believe that, but I don't have to agree he is correct or that the Bible backs up that teaching. Tolerance does not require me to compromise my beliefs. We love people, no matter their lifestyle, no matter what they have done. But we must continue to point them in a better direction, toward God, toward the power that enables them to choose real righteousness. We must never be rude or unkind, and it is never our intention to be hurtful. While we can and should be tolerant, we must also stand for the truth.

This wrong idea about tolerance has led to another concept about truth that is wrong; that is the idea that everyone finds his or her own slant on truth and everybody is right. Look at II Peter 1:20: "Knowing this first, that no prophecy of the scripture is of any private interpretation." There is not one truth for me and another for you. There is only one truth. Let's say someone decides it is only fifty million miles from the earth to the sun. Someone else believes it is 150 million miles to the sun. Now, they can't both be right. In fact, they are both wrong. It is about ninety-three million miles. The Word is the truth, and we must conform our opinions to the Word of God. If one preacher says you are saved by faith alone and another says you must be baptized to be saved, they cannot both be right. And the truth is not affected by either of their opinions. The truth never looks back to see who is following; it just goes on being the truth.

Second, the truth is not only absolute, it is powerful—powerful enough to set men free: "Then said Jesus to those Jews which believed on him, If ye continue in my word, then are ye my disciples indeed; And ye shall know the truth, and the truth shall make you free" (John 8:31–32). Falsehood and compromise cannot liberate; they can only enslave. To declare truth is to break the shackles that hold so many; it is to open the doors to the prison house. It is the *only* key. That is why we must proclaim truth. To do any less may gather a crowd, but will not build a church because people are not set free from sin where there is no truth proclaimed.

Third, the truth opens the way to God. Once Jesus met a woman at Jacob's well in Sychar. After she realized she was speaking to a man with extraordinary insight into the things of God, she asked a question from deep in her heart: "Where can we find God? Some say Jerusalem, some say in a mountain near here, but I need to know. Where can I find Him?" Today, many would tell her that it doesn't matter. God isn't particular about what church or what faith you embrace; after all, all roads lead to God. That most decidedly is *not* what Jesus said. "But the hour cometh, and now is, when the true worshippers shall worship the Father in spirit and in truth: for the Father seeketh such to worship him. God is a Spirit: and they that worship him must worship him in spirit and in truth" (John 4:23–24). The truth is the only route to God. Not feelings, not sacrifice, not good works. Not even the presence of the Spirit alone. There must be truth for humans to find God.

Finally, truth alone will judge us: "Before the LORD: for he cometh, for he cometh to judge the earth: he shall judge the world with righteousness, and the people with his truth" (Psalm 96:13). This is the standard by which all lives will be judged. It is not politically correct; it goes against the modern rejection of anything that smacks of absolutism. Sometimes folks say to us: "Who do you think you are? You think you are right and everyone else is wrong! You are judgmental, and holier–than–thou!" They miss the point. No one will be judged by my opinions or ideas. No one will be judged by what I think the truth is. But they will be judged by what the truth actually is, and the Bible is that truth.

We ourselves as preachers of truth will not be judged by earthly standards of success, but by the truth. Not by the size of our congregations, the prominence of our ministries, the number of those who know our name. We will be judged by the truth: did we preach it, did we live it, did we love it?

> Man with his burning soul
> Has but an hour of breath
> To build a ship of truth
> In which his soul may sail
> Sail on the sea of death
> For death takes toll
> Of beauty, courage, youth,
> Of all but truth.
>
> John Masefield

Sources Cited in Chapter 6

Phillips Brooks, *Lectures On Preaching Delivered Before the Divinity School of Yale College in January and February, 1877* (New York: E. P. Dutton, 1878).

Michael Pollan, *A Place of My Own: The Education of an Amateur Builder* (New York: Bantam Doubleday Dell, 1997).

John Masefield, "Truth" in *The Story of a Round House and Other Poems* (New York: MacMillan, 1912).

Part Three

The Sermon: Preparation

The heights by great men reached and kept
Were not attained by sudden flight,
But they, while their companions slept,
Were toiling upward in the night

Augustine

Preparation precedes power.

Charles Lindbergh

Charles Lindbergh was the first person to fly solo across the Atlantic. He made his historic flight in 1927, after others who had attempted the dangerous flight failed, some losing their lives in the process. Lindbergh succeeded simply because he was better prepared. This devotion to preparation is summed up in the laconic statement often credited to him: "Preparation precedes power."

In no area is this true more than in preaching. An unprepared preacher is a powerless preacher. From time to time there are trends that discount preparation, trends that seem to argue that to prepare is somehow carnal; that to be prepared is to be unable to respond to the Spirit. I think the opposite is true. When I am prepared, my mind is not frantically searching for the words I am to say; instead, it is free to respond to the move of God, knowing that when preaching time comes, I am ready. Prepare well, know what you are going to say, then respond to the Spirit, and you will have power in your preaching.

To step to the pulpit unprepared is one of the most inexcusable behaviors for a preacher. Never accept second best in yourself; always be prepared.

7

THE FIRST STEPS TO PREPARING A SERMON

The less experienced the speaker, the more preparation time is needed. My opinion is, no less than twenty hours for a forty-minute message. The people deserve that. When you multiply the man-hours sitting in your audience (their time), they deserve better than just a few scraps of paper and a cheeseburger Happy Meal.

Stan Gleason

Step One

The first step to being prepared sounds like a simple one: you must decide what you are going to preach. It is only logical that you have to decide what to preach before you can prepare to preach. Of course, it is not as simple as it sounds. It is an act of faith to believe that days before you are to preach, God can direct you to a text and subject that will meet the needs of a congregation. But this is literally true, and you must believe it.

Where do sermon ideas come from? Everywhere: a good story that captures your imagination, a Scripture text that leaps out at you in devotions, a sermon that you read or hear that gets your own mind churning, a newspaper article, something you hear on the radio, or come across on the Internet. Ideas are everywhere. I will never forget Brother Fred Hyde, pastor, missionary, and founder of Spirit of Freedom Ministries, getting a sermon idea from a receipt in a fast food restaurant: "When your order is ready, your number will be called." Be on alert for sermon ideas from everything you read, hear, or see.

Of course, most of your ideas will come from the Bible itself. This makes daily Bible reading vital, not only for personal devotion, but for sermon preparation. The climate, landscape, and culture of the Bible should be as familiar to you as that of the physical world. As you read it, you should be familiar with the basic facts of the who, what, where, when, why, and how of what you read. Watch for the memorable turn of phrase, the striking narrative, the universal application of truth. All these are where sermon thoughts are born.

Step Two

Regardless what catches your attention and captivates your mind, the second step is absolutely crucial: you must write what I call the purpose statement. Some call it the theme, or the thesis. It is one sentence that contains the central idea of the sermon. It should be written down in the beginning when the sermon is still only an idea, it then becomes the measure against which all the subsequently compiled Scriptures, illustrations, and information must be compared. It is the focus that keeps you on track. A fuzzy purpose statement produces a fuzzy sermon. A crisp, clear purpose statement produces a clear sermon. Spend time to get it right. Let's look at some purpose statements I have written and the texts from which they came.

John 1:45–46: "Philip findeth Nathanael, and saith unto him, We have found him, of whom Moses in the law, and the prophets, did write, Jesus of Nazareth, the son of Joseph. And Nathanael said unto him, Can there any good thing come out of Nazareth? Philip saith unto him, Come and see."

My purpose statement: "My purpose is to show that no amount of argument can convince people of the grace and power of Jesus, but if people will 'Come and See' for themselves, they will discover His love for them."

II Kings 7:3–5: "And there were four leprous men at the entering in of the gate: and they said one to another, Why sit we here until we die? If we say, We will enter into the city, then the famine is in the city, and we shall die there: and if we sit still here, we die also. Now therefore come, and let us fall unto the host of the Syrians: if they save us alive, we shall live; and if they kill us, we shall but die. And they rose up in the twilight, to go unto the camp of the Syrians: and when they were come to the uttermost part of the camp of Syria, behold, there was no man there."

My purpose statement: "My purpose is to show that even when we aren't sure of what God will do, if we act on whatever faith we have, rather than surrendering to our doubt, God will respond to our need."

II Samuel 13:1–3 "And it came to pass after this, that Absalom the son of David had a fair sister, whose name was Tamar; and Amnon the son of David loved her. And Amnon was so vexed, that he fell sick for his sister Tamar; for she was a virgin; and Amnon thought it hard for him to do any thing to her. But Amnon had a friend, whose name was Jonadab, the son of Shimeah David's brother: and Jonadab was a very subtil man."

My purpose statement: "My purpose is to convince young people that their destiny can be decided by the people they choose as their friends, since friends will encourage us either to serve God or to turn from Him."

The Third Step

After the purpose statement is written, the next step is the gathering of data. Your sermon is based on a passage of Scripture. You should attempt to learn all you can about that passage. I'll have more to say about this later. Next, identify, by consulting your purpose statement, what application you will be making from this text to the lives of your hearers, and begin collecting information that will illustrate, demonstrate, and illuminate your purpose.

The first source I consult for supporting material for my sermon is the Bible itself. That should be the first choice for content. Why? Because you can never have too much Bible in a sermon! We are called to preach the Word, so put all the Word into your sermons that you reasonably can. I don't mean load it up with dry, arcane theology; rather, use other texts, stories, and events from Scripture to illuminate your topic or theme. Also, remember the purpose of preaching is to convince your hearers of the truth and importance of what you say. Most people you preach to will believe, rightly, that Scripture itself is the arbiter of truth, so use Scripture to support Scripture and demonstrate the truth of your theme.

EXAMPLE SERMON

Let me illustrate the comments I have made so far by looking at a sermon I have constructed and preached. One of my favorite Bible stories is about the four lepers that huddled in the gate of the besieged city of Samaria. The entire story is recorded in II Kings 6–7. I have used this story in many different sermons, but began to see it in a new light when I noticed the remarkable statement: "Why sit we here until we die? If we say, we will enter into the city, then the famine is in the city, and we shall die there: and if we sit still here, we die also. Now therefore come, and let us fall unto the host of the Syrians: if they save us alive, we shall live; and if they kill us, we shall but die" (II Kings 7:3b–4). I saw in my mind's eye as these four desperate men took stock of their situation: a city dying behind them, certain death if they stayed where they were, a ruthless enemy before them. Admitting they had no idea what would be the final outcome, they decided to do the only thing that offered any hope at all—to go to the Syrian camp and see what would happen. I thought about the fact that they were sure of only two things: if they went into Samaria, they would certainly die, and if they stayed where they were, they would also surely die. There was no doubt about the outcome of these two courses of action. The only doubt they had was about the outcome of the only possible action available to them, to go to the Syrian camp: "if they save us alive, we shall live; and if they kill us, we shall but die."

I have noticed many times how people talk themselves out of the blessings of God, because they have some doubt about whether God will actually do for them what they need done. Sometimes, I think, in our efforts to encourage faith, we emphasize the need for it until our hearers draw the conclusion that unless they have total confidence that God will do what they need, He will not hear them. In a way we have an unspoken belief that the least bit of doubt prevents God from responding. This causes discouragement and a resignation to accept less than God would like to do for us.

I do not believe this to be true, and as I studied again this Old Testament story that I had used so many times, I saw it was the perfect text to dispel this tragic mistaken belief that has robbed so many. I wrote the purpose statement you have already read: "My purpose is to show that even when we aren't sure of what

God will do, if we act on whatever faith we have, rather than surrendering to our doubt, God will respond to our need." I have identified what I want to preach, I have located my text, I have written my purpose statement. Now it is time to begin gathering materials to use in the sermon.

After spending more time with the four lepers, I began gathering items about faith and doubt. It quickly became obvious that I would need very little material from outside the Bible itself. I did consult my "sermons preached" database and came across some material I had used in past sermons about education inducing doubt in us by teaching us to question established fact, authority, and convention. I also did some other research and came across information on the widespread acceptance of secular concepts, including evolution, which undermine our faith in the supernatural power of God. But I used Scripture almost exclusively because of the wealth of resources there.

First, there were passages that do what I think of as providing the theology of my theme. Some seemed to support the opposite of my purpose. It is vital not to ignore these, as many of your hearers will know of them or discover them; if you ignore them, it will undermine not only the theme of this sermon, but your credibility as a preacher. I don't mean you need to turn your sermon into a polemical debate or a technical Bible study; I just mean you must present the Bible honestly and openly, giving both sides of the issue. I will talk about this in more detail later. A couple of those verses are Mark 9:23: "Jesus said unto him, 'If thou canst believe, all things are possible to him that believeth,'" and Hebrews 11:6: "But without faith it is impossible to please him: for he that cometh to God must believe that he is, and that he is a rewarder of them that diligently seek him." On the other hand, are these Scriptures: Matthew 17:20 (also Luke 17:6) "And Jesus said unto them, Because of your unbelief: for verily I say unto you, If ye have faith as a grain of mustard seed, ye shall say unto this mountain, Remove hence to yonder place; and it shall remove; and nothing shall be impossible unto you," and Mark 9:24 "And straightway the father of the child cried out, and said with tears, Lord, I believe; help thou mine unbelief."

The real power of the sermon will come from the Bible stories that demonstrate someone receiving from God despite imperfect faith. I made notes on six different events in Scripture that fit my goal:

1. The father bringing his son to Jesus for deliverance (Mark 9)
2. Esther agreeing to go before the king, though it presented an uncertain outcome (Esther 4)
3. The king of Nineveh calling for fasting and repentance, though Jonah never offered any hope (Jonah 9)
4. The leper approaching Jesus for healing, though not sure of the outcome (Matthew 8)
5. The prodigal son returning to his father though unsure whether he would be welcome (Luke 15)

6. The woman of Canaan coming to plead for her daughter's deliverance (Matthew 15)

This seemed to be enough material to build my sermon. In the next two chapters we will talk about how to turn this unorganized mass of information and ideas into a sermon.

In the last chapter, I argued for a determination to preach the Word; this is what you are called to do. Now, let's talk about how to make sure you are doing just that. It begins by devoting yourself to Bible *study*. The Bible is at the heart of the preacher's craft. Devotional reading may inspire sermon topics, but systematic study explores the deeper truths of the Bible, revealing its nuances of structure, text, history, and doctrine, among many other aspects. You should know more about the Bible than anything else: history, sports, hobbies, cars, gardening, construction, politics, or gadgets. It should be your goal to know as much or more about the Word of God than anyone else in your congregation, in your community, in your state. This can only be accomplished by hard, consistent study.

If you were fortunate and blessed enough to have attended Bible college, build on the exposure to the Word you received there. Remember, a college degree, even from a Bible college, does not mean you have arrived; it simply means you have been shown the path and provided with the equipment needed for the journey. How far down the path you go afterward is up to you.

I would urge you to attend one of our Bible colleges, or Urshan College. The systematic approach to learning you encounter there will be invaluable to you. If you cannot, dedicate yourself to self-training. If you can attend a Purpose Institute class, do so without fail. Avail yourself of all the resources available online. One of the best is Ministry Central. All our institutions of higher learning offer distance (online) classes. Be proactive. Your preparation for ministry is ultimately in your hands.

All this begins with your pastor. Most pastors have developed training opportunities for the beginning ministers in the church. Attend these training sessions and place yourself under the mentorship and instruction of your pastor. Remember, the role of your pastor is not just to give you a pulpit to practice your preaching in, it is to develop you spiritually, mentally, and emotionally for the long haul of a life of ministry. Follow his or her instruction and never discount the incredible resource of wisdom, experience, and knowledge God has given you in your pastor. This isn't just smart, it is scriptural. Woe to the beginning preacher who doesn't work under the direction of a pastor! Your ministry will be stillborn.

Start now to build a great library. I prefer a real, physical book in my hands, but I read ebooks, too. The main thing is to buy good books. Quantity is not necessarily quality. One hundred good books are much better than one thousand mediocre ones. The best place to find good books is in the bibliographies of good books. Also, there are books and web pages dedicated to lists and discussions about books focused on the study of the Bible.

Remember, studying the Bible in order to communicate through the medium of preaching is not the same as studying the Bible with an emphasis on simply gaining knowledge about it. Both approaches are valid and vital; just different. You should do both because they overlap. It is much like the difference between a scientist who seeks to gain empirical knowledge without concern for its practical application, and an inventor who uses this pure science, and develops practical applications that we use every day. The researcher seeks truth without worrying whether it will be useful or not. He seeks truth for truth's sake. The inventor takes the pure truth discovered by the researcher and figures out how to utilize it to make a product that will improve everyday life. She seeks truth, not for truth's sake alone, but for what that truth can do.

Recently, I visited the Royal Institute in London. This is the home of the famous laboratories and lecture halls where Humphry Davy and Michael Faraday made and publicly demonstrated some of the most amazing discoveries in science in the early and mid-1800s. I enjoyed the tour of the original area where the labs were and the displays full of the original equipment Davy, Faraday, and others used in their experiments. As I was leaving, I asked the kind lady at the desk if the journals of Michael Faraday were ever put on display. I had long been interested in the famous journals, having read about them for years. They were considered a model of scientific record-keeping. "Well, no," she answered my question, "We have them here in the archives where they have been for the last 175 years. They are considered priceless." I thanked her and again complimented the interesting tour and headed for the door. "Just a minute," she stopped me. "I'll just make a call." Not knowing quite what to expect, I waited as she spoke to someone on the phone. She gave me directions to the subbasement in an area not accessible to the public. "A researcher will be waiting to meet you. She'll be just at the door," she said.

I went down the stairs, and just as the receptionist said, a woman in a white coat waited for me at a large steel door. "Just this way," she said. I followed her into a room with several large tables and desks. A few people worked at the desks. "Now," she said, "I understand you wish to see one of Michael Faraday's journals."

"Absolutely!"

"Do you have any special one in mind?"

"No, I will leave the choice up to you." She disappeared into a vault door in the opposite wall, and in a few minutes, returned with a thin, bound book, much like an old-fashioned ledger. She handed it to me and invited me to sit at one of the tables along the wall behind me and take as long as I liked to examine the book. She walked away, I sat at the table, opened the book in my hands, and I was reading a scientific journal in the handwriting of Michael Faraday. It detailed experiments conducted in 1831–32.

I read through the accounts of several experiments, written in a neat, small hand, and noted the drawings of electromagnets and other equipment, also clearly and precisely done. I soon realized I was reading the original accounts of a scientific discovery that had dramatically changed the world. In 1831 Faraday carefully worked through a series of experiments in which he sought to explore the relationship between electricity and magnetism.

The First Steps to Preparing a Sermon

It had already been discovered that electricity could be made to produce magnetism by wrapping a wire around a piece of metal and introducing an electric current through the wire. The current magnetized the metal as long as it was flowing. Faraday wondered if the opposite could be true: could magnetism produce electricity? In my hands I held the record of the results of those experiments. Faraday passed a magnet through a coil of wire and measured an electric current that resulted from it. He had discovered the principal behind the dynamo, a device that to this day generates the electricity that powers our world. Here, in this manuscript I held in my hands, was his description of a discovery that created the modern world.

In a sense Faraday invented the dynamo, but in another he did not. Others, over the next forty years, turned the researcher's discovery into the forerunners of the powerful machines that we know today. Faraday was a lover of pure science, and in this instance he experimented to learn, but not to apply that learning in a practical way. This is true for the student of the Bible who seeks to know the Word simply for the joy of discovering this fascinating and unique book. We should all be that pure researcher. But preachers should and must go further. As Phillips Brooks explains it:

> So the student preparing to be a preacher cannot learn truth as the mere student of theology for its own sake might do. He always feels it reaching out through him to the people to whom he is some day to carry it. He cannot get rid of this consciousness. It influences all his understanding. We can see

that it must have its dangers. It will threaten the impartiality with which he will seek truth. It will tempt him to prefer those forms of truth which most easily lend themselves to didactic uses, rather than those which bring evidence of being most simply and purely true. That is the danger of all preachers.

Against that danger the man meaning to be a preacher must be upon his guard, but he cannot avoid the danger by sacrificing the habit out of which the danger springs. He must receive truth as one who is to teach it. He cannot, he must not study as if the truth he sought were purely for his own culture or enrichment. And the result of such a habit, followed with due guard against its dangerous tendencies, will be threefold. It will bring, first, a deeper and more solemn sense of responsibility in the search for truth; second, a desire to find the human side of every truth, the point at which every speculation touches humanity; and third, breadth which comes from the constant presence in the mind of the fact that truth has various aspects and presents itself in many ways to different people, according to their needs and characters.

Without Faraday, the inventors would not have known the science that made possible their invention, without the inventors, the science would have remained hidden in a handwritten notebook in the vaults of the Royal Academy. As you study the Bible, look for the applications of its truths, that is, how this ancient but timeless book reveals to us practical truths for our day. Fill your library with good, solid Bible dictionaries, commentaries, Old and New Testament surveys, book studies, doctrinal studies, exegetical studies, character studies, and church histories; and use them to illuminate, explain, and bring to life the eternal truths of the Bible for those who hear you. Remember, the fact that preaching does not have as its primary goal to disseminate information, as does teaching, does not mean it is empty of the deeper truths of God's Word. Those truths are simply offered in a different way: not shallower, but more concise; not altered, but applied.

Now, let's apply all that we have said to the preparation of sermons. You have the sermon's basic idea and you know what you are going to preach. You have written a well-crafted thesis, or purpose statement, so you know what you want to say. Now you turn to your library and its Bible dictionaries, commentaries, and other good books. Don't forget magazines, your favorite Internet resources, as well as your own past sermons. Gather everything you can. The idea is to amass everything that might be useful. Open a folder on your computer or a file in your file cabinet. Put notes on where you found information, scans of book pages, magazine articles, downloads from websites, highlights from ebooks, jotted notes to yourself of ideas for the sermon's structure, notes from phone conversations with friends about the idea, contemporary illustrations, news articles, notes of personal experiences, possible biblical stories that illuminate the sermon: anything and everything that might be used to illustrate your text.

This is where the organization scheme you use to store the information you uncover, run across, dig out, or hear is so important. A maxim to keep in mind is this: if you can't find it when you need it, you might as well not have it. Keep your books organized on the shelf, use color stickers to mark pages with important information. Some people place a sheet of paper in a book, mentioning some important ideas or information and the pages where they can be found. For more sophisticated schemes, there are a multitude of computer programs that catalog books, some with searchable fields to record important highlights. Some are inexpensive, some are expensive, depending on the program's capabilities. Scans of pages from books, downloaded documents, highlights from ebooks, notes of past sermons, sermons in development, or simply random ideas, can all be simply stored in computer folders by subject, and searched by keywords or any word. On the more advanced side, but with a steeper learning curve, are free-form database programs that can keep track of any number of variables and provide even more flexibility. I use essentially two programs, Evernote and Paperport.

The important thing is, whatever method you use to maintain your data must actually be used, or it is worthless. No matter how sophisticated your software, unless you catalog your books, scan magazine articles, and import your notes and outlines, it is a waste of money. It must become your habit to maintain your data, keeping it at your fingertips. This is why a simple plan that you will use is better than a sophisticated plan you won't, and why I recommend you start with something simple and move on from there.

As you are gathering data, don't forget the simple examination of the text. This will help prevent the most common mistake novice (and sometimes experienced) preachers make: using Scripture out of context or otherwise mistaking its true meaning. An otherwise great preacher once misread Proverbs 13:20. The text reads: "He that walketh with wise men shall be wise: but a companion of fools shall be destroyed." Somehow he read the word "companion" as "champion" and prepared and preached a sermon about people who excuse, or "take up for" fools and their words and behavior, in other words a "champion" of fools. He told me that all through the sermon people seemed at first confused, then amused (a deadly combination for a preacher to inspire in a congregation). Later someone kindly pointed out his mistake. He told me about his embarrassment and said, "I wish I would have just read it one more time!"

In order to avoid such easily made mistakes, you should ask yourself a few questions about every passage of Scripture you plan to use in your sermon, whether it is your "text" or not:

1. Who is the speaker? For instance, are we hearing from God or the devil; a prophet or an infidel?
2. Who is being spoken to?
3. What is the occasion?
4. Where is all this happening?

5. Why?
6. What is the application for us?

I asked these questions of all the Bible stories and Scripture verses I gathered for the sermon we have discussed in this chapter. As you will see, they helped determine which ones I would use and which ones I would save for another day.

The Fourth Step

The fourth step is the honing of materials. By that I mean deciding what to use and not to use in the sermon. Ideally, you will have more content than you could preach in one sermon. Start the process by referring to the purpose statement. This is the ruler you will use to decide what to use and what to file away for future reference. Be ruthless: any illustration, Bible story, or character development that does not fit, get rid of it. Anything that does not propel the sermon forward to its closing, anything that doesn't point your hearers directly to your purpose, get rid of it. Hone, sharpen the focus, keep only that which fits like a glove. Remember, there will always come a time to use the other information. Keep your eye on the goal.

Sometimes things may fit just fine, but there is too much for one sermon. Sometimes things have to be culled, not because they aren't good, or because they aren't a great fit, but because you don't have the time to use them. You can only preach so long.

This is probably a good time to talk about sermon length. How long should you preach? The simple answer is until

The First Steps to Preparing a Sermon

you are done. The better answer is until your congregation is done. Take it from a preacher who has preached the Spirit down, only to preach it back up again more times than I care to admit, it's better to stop too soon than too late. Remember, the purpose of preaching is not to show how knowledgeable you are or to overwhelm your hearers with unassailable proofs piled one upon the other. The purpose of preaching is to bring people to the point of a response to the Word of God. This is a delicate calculus, a balance between the power of the Word, and the Spirit. Learn to recognize the moving of the Spirit and move in that flow.

Acceptable sermon length changes over time. When I was a teenager, no sermon was under an hour, and many were much longer. I have listened to two-hour-plus sermons. When I began preaching, the feeling was if you didn't preach an hour you weren't trying. Over time, attention spans have shortened, and now, although not unusual, hour-long sermons are not the rule.

Personally, I try to be completely done (including acknowledging the introduction, thanking whoever invited me to preach, recognizing special guests, preaching, and giving the altar appeal) within forty-five minutes. This means the sermon itself needs to be thirty to forty minutes max. As a beginning preacher, preach twenty to thirty minutes, no more.

This requires careful use of your materials to provide a sermon that moves quickly without haste, covers the subject adequately without bogging down, and moves people to respond in prayer and worship at the end. Not an easy task! You must carefully choose from the materials you have gathered, then skillfully weave together what you have chosen to create an effective sermon.

If you hope to do this, you must become effective at gauging the emotional impact of each of the materials you have gathered. You must answer these questions: How forcefully will this Scripture verse, story, or illustration drive home my point? How much emotion will it create in the hearts of my hearers? And, how effectively will it propel my hearers toward a response to the presence of God?

SERMON EXAMPLE

Let's look again at the sermon we have been working on. Of the six stories I found, which one do you think has the most emotional impact? Here they are again:

1. The father bringing his son to Jesus for deliverance (Mark 9)
2. Esther agreeing to go before the king, though it presented an uncertain outcome (Esther 4)
3. The king of Nineveh calling for fasting and repentance, though Jonah never offered any hope (Jonah 9)
4. The leper approaching Jesus for healing, though not sure of the outcome (Matthew 8)
5. The prodigal son returning to his father though unsure whether he would be welcome (Luke 15)
6. The woman of Canaan coming to plead for her daughter's deliverance (Matthew 15)

What would be your choice? For me, the story with the most impact is the story of the father who brought his demon-possessed son to Jesus. He is obviously shattered, at his wits end, and overwhelmed by the suffering of his son. This innocent child presents a heart-rending picture; no one can remain unmoved by this desperate father and his tormented son. I have something special in mind for this story.

How would you rate, in order, the emotional impact of the rest of the stories, the most impactful to the least? This determines how you will fit them into your sermon to create an emotional current, carrying your congregation toward the closing and the altar.

Here is my list:

1. Father and demon-possessed son come to Jesus.
2. Four lepers march on the Syrians.
3. King of Nineveh repents.
4. Esther goes to the throne room.
5. Prodigal son comes home.
6. Woman of Canaan asks for the crumbs.

Normally, I would discard all but the first three. Since each of those three needs some background and detail in order to maximize its impact, to try to do more, along with an introduction and a closing, is to risk going too long.

Discarding number six, the woman of Canaan, is not hard since it doesn't really fit anyway: Jesus Himself said she had "great faith," and since we are trying to

> reach those who have little faith, we will save her for another time. But I really like the two that are left, Esther and the prodigal son, and I may have an idea how we can effectively work in Esther and the prodigal son too, without going over time.

I'll show you how in the next chapter. First let's look at types of sermons and why it is important to recognize the type of sermon you are going to preach.

Sources Cited in Chapter 7

Phillips Brooks, *Lectures On Preaching Delivered Before the Divinity School of Yale College in January and February, 1877* (New York: E. P. Dutton, 1878).

8

WHAT TYPE OF SERMON IS IT?

The classification of sermons is a topic that seems to capture the attention of many preachers and those who write about preaching. Many schemes have been proposed, some are detailed and elaborate, and some are simple and straightforward. While I believe it is important to keep in mind a general idea of the genre of your sermon, most of what you need to know is found in the purpose statement itself. More than just stating the theme or thesis, a purpose statement also helps keep you focused on those who will hear your sermon, not just on the sermon itself. This is more important than fitting a sermon into a certain category. A second reason I think the classification of sermons can be overemphasized is that most sermons are not just one type, but often display characteristics of several types at once, fitting neatly into no one category.

Having said that, though, it is good to at least become familiar with the concept of thinking of sermons in categories, for the simple reason that identifying the prevalent category of a sermon is a tool that can clarify your thinking and thereby help you preach a more effective sermon. For example, if you know the aim of your sermon is evangelistic (aimed at those who are unsaved), then this knowledge would help you craft your opening and certainly your closing. It could also affect your choice of materials, as how you select them will be guided by the fact your target audience will probably be less familiar with the Bible, especially its doctrine and terminology, than saints will be. When you preach to the church, you can make certain assumptions about what they already know and don't know, but when you preach to the lost you must assume that their knowledge of the Bible is limited. You should avoid difficult theological terms, church jargon, and other language with which they may be unfamiliar. Other classifications will have a similar effect on how you craft your sermon.

There are as many ways to classify sermons as there are books and authors on the preaching of sermons.

W. E. Sangster, in *The Craft of the Sermon*, offers a classification system with six classes:

1. Biblical interpretation
2. Ethical and devotional
3. Doctrinal
4. Apologetic

5. Social
6. Evangelistic

Brown, Clinard, and Northcutt, in *Steps to the Sermon*, another classic work in the field, identify seven classes:

1. Expository
2. Biblical
3. Analytical
4. Contemporary
5. Special Forms
6. Occasional
7. Evangelistic

A more modern approach is found in *The Art and Craft of Biblical Preaching*, edited by Haddon Robinson and Craig Brian Larson. The authors of this book seem to emphasize seven genres of sermons:

1. Expository (defined as revealing the meaning of a Scripture passage and applying that meaning to the hearer's life)
2. Verse by verse (really a subgenre of expository preaching)
3. Textual (defined as being based on a shorter passage than expository)
4. Topical (sometimes I have heard this called "thought" preaching, and it is probably the most common among Pentecostals)
5. Series of sermons

6. First-person narrative (telling a Bible story from the viewpoint of one of its characters)
7. Evangelistic

John A. Broadus, in his classic work *On the Preparation and Delivery of Sermons,* classifies sermons based on homiletical structure, content, and pattern. The only category relevant to the present discussion, however, is the first: homiletical structure. He further divides this category into four genres:

1. Textual
2. Topical
3. Textual-Topical
4. Expository

These are just a few of the approaches to classifying sermons that have been devised over the centuries; all of them have something to commend them. If you have an interest, you can read all the sources I have mentioned and many, many more, and there certainly may be benefit in doing this. But I am a simple preacher, and for the purposes of this book, let's think of sermon classes in a simpler way, even more simply than Broadus does.

In a practical and empirical way, a sermon is either aimed toward the saved, or it is aimed toward the lost. For our purposes, this is the most basic way to think of the sermon, and has the most impact on its structure and content. The decision whether the sermon is evangelistic or not is one of the first you must make while in the process of crafting it.

This decision must be and will be reflected in your purpose statement.

Now a word of caution that complicates things: we have all preached sermons that were intended for the church, but that under the unction of the Holy Spirit were transformed into evangelistic appeals. We have also seen the opposite happen. In fact, most of us, in every sermon, regardless of its classification, structure, or subject matter, include an evangelistic appeal at some point, or in the case of a predominantly evangelistic sermon, include the needs of the saved people who are there by alluding to healing, or supernatural help with family, marital, or financial issues. This is not bad or wrong, or to be avoided, but is simply a fundamental part of preaching to congregations that are growing and dynamic and thus include people with many needs. Such churches most always have people on the pews that need to respond to the call of God in their lives for salvation, as well as church members who are dealing with many other needs. Pastors who are blessed to preach to such congregations can't well afford to ignore the motivational, doctrinal, or devotional types of sermons, but also must learn to employ the techniques of the evangelistic sermon, often within the same sermon.

So, when building sermons, we should think of them as having a *predominant* genre or classification; namely, either they are predominantly evangelistic or predominately to benefit the church. If a sermon is predominantly evangelistic, for example, and you wish to include the church in your target audience, it is important that you do so in a smooth and logical way. Find a *hook* in your material that restates your purpose in a way that addresses the needs of the saved. Utilize a Bible story, an illustration, or a Scripture verse to do this.

> **SERMON EXAMPLE**
>
> In the sermon we have been working on, most of the stories that we intend to use are targeted toward saved people, as is our overall purpose. The story of the father and his demon- possessed son appeals to those that are saved and, like that father, are coming to Jesus for healing or deliverance. The story of Esther is about a member of the king's household coming before the throne, so this too is more targeted toward those that are saved. The story of the four lepers is also more about those who are already saved and in need of a miracle.
>
> However, the story of the king of Nineveh who, without even hearing about repentance, repented, and ordered the entire city to repent, is obviously a great *hook* for including those who need to come to God. The story of the prodigal son provides an opportunity to encourage those who are backslidden to come back home again even if they're not sure of the welcome they would receive.
>
> So, even though this sermon will mainly deal with people who are saved but struggle with the fear that their faith is not strong enough to bring God's answer to their needs, there are a couple of hooks that, if used well, can open the appeal to both the backslider and those who have never known God.

What Type of Sermon Is It?

By keeping firmly in mind the primary target audience for the sermon, we avoid what to me is a recurring weakness in many of the classification systems that have been devised. That is, they mix and overlap sermon types. For example, three of the four examples I gave you above list "evangelistic" as one of the classes. Yet with one minor exception ("occasional" in Brown et al.) all the other classes they list are based on the *structure* or *technique* of the sermon, and have nothing to do with its purpose. "Evangelistic" has everything to do with the purpose of the sermon, that is, *who* you intend to reach and the *response* you want from them. I think this mixing of types or classes causes unnecessary confusion, and leads to giving up on the whole idea of considering the classification of one's sermons. By settling early in the process, and then keeping your eye on, who you are predominantly trying to reach, you can use the consideration of the classification of your sermon to avoid a mixed up mess and help keep your preaching crystal clear.

You will notice that all the other classes will fit under both categories of saved or lost. A textual sermon will work equally well under either category, as will topical, expository, or most any other category. The important thing is to stay focused on your target audience and allow whatever technique or structure you use to bring them to a place of response to the message.

Now, let's look at two major types of sermons based on technique or structure. If you understand these types, the differences between them, and how to master them, you will have a much better understanding of how to put a sermon together. Almost all the other types are subtypes of these two.

Expository Preaching

First, let's look at expository preaching. As defined above, this is "revealing the meaning of a Scripture passage and applying that meaning to the hearer's life." The emphasis here is on the passage of Scripture itself. All of the materials gathered, other texts, illustrations, and definitions, serve only to explain and reinforce the message of the text you are expounding. Your sermon may be focused on one verse, a dozen verses, or an entire chapter, but for that sermon those are your entire world. No theme or subject is introduced that is not found in that passage. This is "Bible preaching" in its purest form. Subforms are verse-by-verse preaching and series preaching. While all preaching should be grounded in the Scripture, expository preaching is the most grounded of all.

William Sangster gives four reasons preaching the Bible in this way has benefits beyond the simple fact that there is unlimited power in preaching the unadorned Word of God. The first is that expository preaching offers endless material for the preacher to preach. I once was in the home of a pastor who told me that for the preceding eleven years he had been preaching through the Book of Proverbs. He told me that he was on chapter 13 and was not sure he would live long enough to finish the book. The expository preacher never lacks something to preach.

Another advantage that Sangster mentions is expository preaching keeps preachers on guard against their own biases.

All of us have our favorite topics to preach, and often in the press of the busy pastorate, or under the demands of the bivocational lifestyle, we fall into the habit of preaching the things we are most familiar with, or most comfortable with, or those topics that speak more into our own hearts. By preaching systematically through a chapter or a book, we are guaranteeing that we will avoid the trap of staying in our comfort zone, or preaching to our own needs, rather than those of our hearers.

Third, Sangster speaks of the fact that preaching expository sermons encourages those who hear us to study the Bible for themselves. I would add that it highlights the Bible in the minds of our congregation and creates a climate of love for God's Word. Traveling and preaching in churches across the United Pentecostal Church International, I've often been able to discern the kind of preaching ministry the pastor offers. Those who preach with a focus on the Bible, making it not only the text of their sermons, but allowing it to speak clearly through expository preaching, are more likely to produce a congregation with a love for the Word of God, an open heart to God's Word, and a thirst and hunger to hear more about the Word of God. Congregations usually value what their pastor values.

Finally, Sangster points out that a preacher cannot dodge the difficult when preaching systematically through a portion of the Word. Certain difficult subjects that we might tend to avoid may be handled more diplomatically, and even more effectively, when they are embedded in a passage along with many other less painful subjects. When I pastored, I often found that using the Word Aflame Sunday school literature, rather than lessons I wrote from scratch, offered me the same benefit. Everyone knew I was just following the "quarterly," so I wasn't singling out anyone, or any situation. I often marveled how lessons that had been written several years before came at the right time for my congregation. The same is true when preaching through a book or a lengthy passage. You will often be amazed at how God can take your preaching and address situations and circumstances in your congregation through the flow of the Word of God.

This type of Bible preaching is not as easy as musing publicly about our own opinions and ideas. It is a challenge because, done right, it requires long hours of deep study. On the other hand, every moment spent preparing a sermon that is full of the Word of God has a great reward, both to the preacher who prepares it and to the hearer. Feed your hearers on a steady diet of God's Word. Avoid the temptation of the trivial, offering shallow preaching based on the latest trends, faddish ideas, empty rhetoric, and worn-out examples. Get into the Word for yourself and get it deep in your own heart. It will not only bless your life, but, when you share it under the anointing of God, you will bless the lives of your hearers like nothing else could possibly do.

Topical Preaching

Topical preaching, sometimes called "thought" or devotional preaching is the second category that I wish to mention. By the foregoing discussion of the importance and power of expository preaching, I do not mean to denigrate or demean topical preaching. On the contrary, done well, topical preaching is just as much focused on Scripture as expository; it simply uses the Word in a different way. By applying many different texts to a unifying theme or "thought," topical preaching focuses the Word of God on the challenges and struggles of everyday life in the twenty-first century in a thought-provoking and inspirational way.

The Bible is a living book. Some have interpreted this to mean that its plain admonitions and teachings are plastic, molded by changing culture, society, and circumstance to fit whatever belief is current in our day. Nothing could be further from the truth. "Thy word is forever settled in heaven," the psalmist said (Psalm 119:89). The Word of God is not made malleable by circumstances or by cultural changes. The Word of God is inviolate; it is a firm foundation. But this firm foundation fits modern life as well as it fit life when it was first penned. The Word of God contains principles that apply to any time and to any place. It offers help in any of the circumstances and situations in life. Preaching the Word of God in our time is the great challenge of the pulpit today. It involves, above all, making clear those eternal principles which do not change and are forever relevant. This is the great work of the modern-day preacher; it is the hardest work that he or she will ever face.

Fidelity to the Word of God is an absolute must for the Pentecostal preacher. To stray from the plain teachings of the Bible in order to claim relevance to our changing culture is the cardinal error for any of us. To preach the plain truths of the Bible is an absolute must if we are to accomplish the purpose of God. Yet even in this modern world filled with problems, we must present those truths in a way that is relevant and reaches the hearts of our hearers.

Topical preaching is a tool that connects the Word of God to circumstances that people face today. Preaching such sermons is sometimes described as shallow, but it certainly need not be, indeed, must not be. To rally people, to instill courage in them in a time of trouble, to put faith and strength into a flagging spirit, are not only some of the most rewarding accomplishments of preaching, but are absolutely essential in a confusing world like the one in which we live. Devotional preaching is necessary for a pastor or other minister who stands before people whose whole week is filled with disappointment and heartache, people who come to church desperately searching for a word from God that will give them the courage to face another day.

Thankfully, the Word of God does not fail us in this challenge. It is filled with the stories of those who overcame, who have endured, indeed, who have triumphed. Their stories are in God's Word, not simply for entertainment, but for inspiration. And those stories are as valuable today as they have ever been. Sometimes I think we miss the boat when we grow tired of stories we've heard all of our lives, when those stories have lost their impact on us because of their familiarity, and we forget that many who walk into our churches have never heard those stories preached under the anointing of God and applied to modern-day life.

EXAMPLE SERMON

The sermon we have been putting together is a topical sermon, primarily directed toward the church, although we will also appeal to those who need renewing and those who need the Holy Spirit baptism. The topic is faith. We are attempting to answer the question: must we have absolutely no doubt that God will answer our prayer in order for God to do so?

This is a vital topic, striking to the core of living for God, and much on the minds of those who have needs that only God can meet. The stories we will use to inspire and encourage are well-known, but we will be preaching them from a slightly different angle than they are usually preached, and we hope this will make them as fresh and exciting as they would be if they were new.

Evangelistic Preaching

In the final section of this chapter, I would like to share a word about preaching to the lost. Evangelistic preaching is, in one sense, a redundancy. While there can be preaching without evangelism, there can be no evangelism without preaching. That this is true is made clear by Romans 10:13–15:

> For whosoever shall call upon the name of the Lord shall be saved. How then shall they call on him in whom they have not believed? and how shall they believe in him of whom they have not heard? and how shall they hear without a preacher? And

> how shall they preach, except they be sent? as it is written, How beautiful are the feet of them that preach the gospel of peace, and bring glad tidings of good things!

In another sense, though, it is a perfectly good term because it differentiates between preaching that is aimed at presenting salvation to those who have never known the Lord and preaching aimed in other directions, such as training or encouraging those already saved. While most good sermons will address several needs, both of the saved and the lost, evangelistic preaching is a method of presenting truth that is especially focused on the lost.

First, let's consider what we mean by evangelistic. In the most precise sense, evangelism is the proclamation of the gospel. The English word *evangel* is simply a transliteration of the Greek word *euangelion*, meaning "good tidings or good news." *Gospel*, which is a contraction of the Anglo-Saxon word *godspell*, has the same meaning.

For those of us who know the truth, evangelism must always hold the meaning of not just proclaiming the gospel, but creating the atmosphere in which souls can meet Jesus in the full power of His Spirit, and follow His example and command in baptism. Anything less is not true evangelistic preaching. So, what about door-knocking, home Bible studies, or street services? Aren't these evangelism? Certainly, they are. But the aim of each of them is to bring people to a point of hunger, or at the least, curiosity about the gospel. When they respond and come into an atmosphere created by Bible preaching, the work of evangelizing them is completed by the preaching and their response to it.

One could think of the difference between preaching to the lost and preaching to the church much like the difference between communicating within a family and communicating with guests in your home. When it's just the family, there may be reference to events, jokes, and family secrets that everyone in the family is familiar with. When you have guests, however, you have to explain such references or risk leaving your guests in the dark, not understanding what you are talking about. This is like the difference between an evangelistic sermon and a sermon that is geared toward the needs of the church. The evangelistic sermon assumes the hearers don't understand church jargon, terms, events, and doctrines. It does not require an introductory course to understand; it is the gospel presented simply, in everyday language, so that the uninitiated can easily understand what they must do to be saved.

This does not mean an evangelistic sermon has no doctrine, avoids biblical concepts, or uses first-grade English. You should not insult your audience in such a way. If I wander into a session at a conference for brain surgeons and I don't understand everything they are talking about, it does not mean I am an ignoramus. It means I am not familiar with the subject. Most people today are not familiar with the Bible, the need for salvation, and the plan God has for their lives both here and in the hereafter. Evangelistic preaching seeks to meet people where they are and bring them to faith and obedience to the gospel so that they might be saved.

Evangelistic preaching could be considered as being rooted in Philippians 4:19: "But my God shall supply all your need according to his riches in glory by Christ Jesus." Let's look at this statement in some detail.

You have a need. This is the first job of the evangelist: to point out the need of the sinner. In our day many come to our churches who require little reminding of their needs. They are broken and shattered by sin, and have often tried many things to meet their needs. All they have tried has failed, and the result for most of them is only to have made their lives worse. They are ready for help. But, you should still point out their needs. Talk to them about what is happening in their lives. Remind them of the false promise of the world. In doing so, try to maintain as broad an appeal as possible. Mention a broad range of specific sins, or better yet, speak in broad terms, not to avoid naming sin, but to be sure everyone feels you are speaking to them.

I have a God. The second job of an evangelistic sermon is to tell them about our God, who alone can meet their needs. A brilliant example of this simple but vital aspect of reaching the lost is Paul's sermon in Acts 17:22–28:

> Then Paul stood in the midst of Mars' hill, and said, Ye men of Athens, I perceive that in all things ye are too superstitious. For as I passed by, and beheld your devotions, I found an altar with this inscription, TO THE UNKNOWN GOD. Whom therefore ye ignorantly worship, him declare I unto you. God that made the world and all things therein, seeing that he is Lord of heaven

and earth, dwelleth not in temples made with hands; Neither is worshipped with men's hands, as though he needed any thing, seeing he giveth to all life, and breath, and all things; And hath made of one blood all nations of men for to dwell on all the face of the earth, and hath determined the times before appointed, and the bounds of their habitation; That they should seek the Lord, if haply they might feel after him, and find him, though he be not far from every one of us: For in him we live, and move, and have our being; as certain also of your own poets have said, For we are also his offspring.

Paul didn't condemn, or even debate their idolatry; he simply used their own superstitions to point them to the only God who made them, loves them as His children, and is near them to hear their prayers. Don't forget to assure them that not only *can* He meet their needs, but He *will*. No one is too bad, too sinful, too far gone. Tell them His mercy is abundant, His power unlimited, His love so great He is moved by our needs; and if we come to Him, He will receive us.

Third, always lift up Jesus. "And I, if I be lifted up from the earth, will draw all men unto me" (John 12:32). He is speaking of His death on the cross. The Cross is the source of this hope and confidence. Don't be afraid of John 3:16 because it is not Acts 2:38; it is still true and offers no contradiction when one understands what is involved when someone "believeth on Him." God came in the form of a man, died for our sins, and now anyone who believes and obeys can be saved.

Finally, preach for a response. The first Pentecostal sermon was an evangelistic sermon. It was deliberately designed under the anointing of God to bring its hearers to a point of action. Peter ended this gem with a powerful closing, specifically targeting his Jewish hearers:

> This Jesus hath God raised up, whereof we all are witnesses. Therefore being by the right hand of God exalted, and having received of the Father the promise of the Holy Ghost, he hath shed forth this, which ye now see and hear. For David is not ascended into the heavens: but he saith himself, The LORD said unto my Lord, Sit thou on my right hand, until I make thy foes thy footstool. Therefore let all the house of Israel know assuredly, that God hath made that same Jesus, whom ye have crucified, both Lord and Christ! (Acts 2:32–36).

When Peter closed his message with these words, full of both accusation and hope, we can only imagine the scene. Perhaps silence falls across the crowd as each hearer comes face to face with his guilt before God. Then, we witness for the first time, the power of the preaching of the gospel by a Holy Ghost–filled preacher under the anointing of the Spirit:

> Now when they heard this, they were pricked in their heart, and said unto Peter and to the rest of the apostles, Men and brethren, what shall we do? Then Peter said unto them, Repent, and be baptized every one of you in the name of Jesus Christ for the remission of sins, and ye shall receive the gift of the Holy Ghost. For the promise is unto you, and to your children, and to all that are afar off, even as many as the Lord our God shall call. And with many other words did he testify and exhort, saying, Save yourselves from this untoward generation. Then they that gladly received his word were baptized: and the same day there were added unto them about three thousand souls (Acts 2:37–41).

May all your preaching have such an effect!

Let me end with a word to beginning preachers. Master the evangelistic sermon. Master it by committing yourself to preaching evangelistically. You will be sorely tempted in your preaching to focus on the church, particularly to point out their shortcomings and failures. Resist this temptation at all costs! You don't have the chops to preach that kind of sermon yet, at least in a way that anyone will accept as any more than the words of a novice. Take to heart instead the words of instruction that the apostle Paul gave to a young preacher: "Do the work of an evangelist" (II Timothy 4:5). If you will learn to compassionately and creatively point out the need of those who do not know the Lord, remind them of the mercy and grace of Jesus, constantly lift Him up, and learn to close your sermons by creating a climate where the Holy Ghost can move into the service and convict the hearts of those who hear you, you will make a place for your ministry, and, more important, you will be a blessing to all those to whom you preach.

Sources Cited in Chapter 8

William E. Sangster, *The Craft of Sermon Construction* (Philadelphia: Westminster Press, 1950, 1951).

H. C. Brown, Jr., H. Gordon Clinard, Jesse J. Northcutt, *Steps to the Sermon* (Nashville: Broadman Press, 1963).

Haddon Robinson and Craig Brian Larson, eds., *The Art and Craft of Biblical Preaching* (Grand Rapids: Zondervan, 2005).

John A. Broadus, *On The Preparation and Delivery of Sermons* 4th ed. (New York: Harper Collins, 1979).

9

PUTTING IT ALL TOGETHER

> Don't just throw the seed at the people! Grind it into flour, bake it into bread, and slice it for them!
>
> Charles Haddon Spurgeon

Now it is time to take all we have discussed and commit the sermon to paper. Keep the purpose statement firmly in mind as you begin creating your introduction, arranging your materials, and crafting the closing. Keep an eye on whether you will mainly reach for the lost or seek to encourage and challenge the saints (unless you are a novice, in which case you should keep your eye on the lost). So how do you put a sermon together?

A sermon is usually thought of as having three basic parts: the introduction, the body, and the closing. Keeping this in mind will help you construct tight, easily-understood sermons. The most important and difficult parts are the introduction and the closing, each of them requiring real skill to make them effective. Let's look at each of these three parts.

The Introduction

If you watch great preachers preach, you'll soon become aware that they all pay great attention to how they begin their sermons. No matter what technique they use, they are meticulous in putting the introduction together. Many of them read their introductions verbatim from their notes, rhythmically turning the pages (or sliding their finger across the screen of their tablet), carefully enunciating the words, dramatically demanding we follow them into the world of their message. What do they know that requires such an obvious investment in time and energy? Why is the introduction so important? They know that there is only a limited time, probably less than two minutes, to get your hearers' attention and convince them you have something to say worth saying.

In his book *You Are the Message*, Roger Ailes insists when you engage an individual or an audience you have only seven seconds to convince them you and your opinions are worth their time. If you think about it, you will realize he is probably right. Around a restaurant table, in the display hall at general conference, in a seminar, at church, everyone subconsciously and quickly "does the math" about whoever is talking and gives their attention or tunes them out. Their decision is based on many shadowy factors, including physical appearance, what is said, how it is said, past interactions with the individual, as well as how well that person adheres to social conventions that create a comfort zone around him or her. In other words, loud, rude airheads don't command our attention; instead, we instinctively try to find an escape route, even if it is just retreating into our own heads when we can't physically get away.

To be fair, a Pentecostal congregation will give you more than seven seconds, mainly because they came to church to hear good preaching, so they are rooting for you. They will give you a chance if for no other reason than they hope not to be bored to death, but they won't give you much more than those seven seconds. So pay attention to how you begin.

(For the following discussion of the parts of a sermon I am indebted to *Introduction to Homiletics* by Donald E. Demaray. As its title suggests, this work is a basic and simply-presented book on preaching that I have read and referred to many times.)

The great Roman orator, Cicero, wrote that all effective introductions must fulfill three purposes: to arouse interest, to secure favor, and to prepare to lead. As in the case with Aristotle's three proofs, no one has improved on this description very much. What did Cicero mean? Arousing interest is pretty clear: if you don't get the congregation's attention in the beginning, you probably won't get it at all, and the rest of the sermon will fall flat. To secure favor means to create a bond between you and the audience, putting them at ease with you, assuring them that not only do you have something to say, but that you know what you are talking about. The third one is a little harder to nail down. One reason is that, to me, it is connected to and flows out of the second one, securing favor. Once you have gained their attention and put them at ease with you, you must draw them into the sermon, causing them to trust that you know where you are going, and then lead them into the body of your sermon and on to the closing.

Arousing Interest

In order to arouse interest, a carefully-thought-out opening sentence is vital. It must catch their attention away from every distraction in the room: bodies settling into seats, scraping of chairs, even the sudden absence of background music, a silence that can be so loud. After pausing a beat to let things settle, read your text, announce your title, then begin your opening with that first sentence. Demand the crowd's attention by clearly presenting its arresting statements and assertions. This first sentence is vital, so prepare it with care. Mull it over in your mind, frame it on paper, reframe it, and revise it as many times as necessary. Perfect it for interest and clarity, and deliver it with confidence.

After the first sentence, set your rhythm. Follow with a second sentence that expands, explains, or elucidates the first one. As you move through the opening paragraph, draw them in by making it personal. Remember your purpose statement; consider the question, why does it matter to them? *Tell* them why it matters in simple, active verbs and concrete nouns. Establish the momentum and keep it going. Remember, the whole of the introduction must arouse interest. It is during those first two minutes or so that the audience makes that all important decision—whether or not to listen to what you have to say.

Someone has said there are three kinds of preachers: those you cannot listen to, those you can listen to, and those you must listen to. People don't come expecting the first; either they come with the intention to listen or they don't come to church at all. For most, option two is the best they can hope for, and probably what they expect. Your job in those first few moments is to persuade them to opt for number three: make it so interesting they simply *must* listen.

Securing Favor

Securing favor also must happen quickly, or not at all. If you are preaching in a familiar church, particularly at home, people already know you and hopefully like and accept you as a preacher. If you are preaching in an unfamiliar setting, you must draw people to you and create a bond between you and the audience. Sometimes this bonding is hard to define. I think this is so because it is an impression, almost an emotion, that your hearers feel rather than think, and this impression is the result of many things. Your appearance—muted, modest, conservative dress; confidence rather than nervousness; assurance of the importance of what you are about to preach; but not arrogance, aloofness, or stiffness—plays a great part in creating this. The tone of your voice—low, yet vibrant; real, almost conversational in the beginning as you politely acknowledge the invitation that brought you to that pulpit—speaks more than your words to the congregation. A gracious manner—complimenting the pastor and the music, a kind word about the worship of the church—is another clue that the congregation will use to size you up.

Humor is a great tool to gain favor, but it must be used carefully and sparingly, particularly when you are preaching to an unfamiliar audience. Nothing that can remotely be interpreted as off-color, derogatory, or disrespectful will work, except to dig a hole you may not get out of. Obvious jokes rarely work either (except for a well-known television preacher whose shtick includes a usually corny joke that works because it is anticipated by his sympathetic crowd). Humor should be connected to relevant situations. Often the kind words of the person that introduced you can be a starting point: "Wow, now I *am* the most over-introduced preacher in Pentecost!" or "Thank you for all those kind words! I probably shouldn't have heard all that, but I'm sure glad my spouse did!"

People love to be complimented, so look for something you can honestly say something nice about—the décor, the choir, the praise team, the nice basket in your room—be sincere and don't overdo it, and it will help win their favor. Above all, be real and always focus their attention on the presence of the Lord. This is the true bond between you and the congregation; they want to know that you know Him, love Him, and will lead them to Him.

Prepare to Lead

The third purpose of the introduction, according to Cicero, is to prepare to lead. People come to church with their minds distracted and scattered. They are impossible to lead until you have gained their attention and won their confidence. Once you have done this, then lead them into the Scripture and into your sermon.

People follow confident leaders; leaders who know who they are and where they are going. You must project both of these characteristics in order to lead them. These cannot be faked, your hearers will quickly sense if you are not ready to lead them, and they will hold back. Don't flail around, starting and stopping, repeating yourself, obviously struggling to get going. Once you have read your text in a smooth, confident way; stated your opening line with a sureness that comes from that confidence, let the introduction and then the body of the sermon unfold. In this way you will lead them where you have been led by the Word and the Spirit. This is why your introduction needs to be well-thought-out and well-crafted; you must first know where you are going in order to lead others there.

AN EXAMPLE INTRODUCTION
Romans 10

The epistle to the Romans was written by Paul around AD 58. The church in Rome was mostly Gentile by the time of the epistle's writing, but it was founded by Jewish Christians. And there are many Jews still there, in spite of imperial edicts banishing Jews from Rome. Paul is introducing himself to this church which, although he seems to know several of its members, he has never visited. He is also hoping to enlist the church's support for his future missionary work. The theme of the letter, according to David Bernard, is "The gospel of salvation is the gift of God's righteousness received by faith in Jesus Christ."

Prior to chapter 10, Paul has already affirmed the doctrine of universal guilt, that "all have sinned and come short of the glory of God" (Romans 3:23), and, beginning in chapter 9, he focuses on Israel, specifically addressing the question, why, if they are the chosen people of God, is Israel lost? Paul Achtemeier points out he does this by asserting what is the theme of the entire chapter "It is not as though the word of God has failed" (Romans 9:6). Now, in chapter 10, he begins his argument as to why, if God's word has not failed, Israel is still lost. His conclusion is that it is because they have refused to hear.

Romans 10 is a stand-alone rhetorical piece developing this argument. We can see it as a sermon following ancient rules of rhetoric; for example, it is a blend of judicial and deliberative rhetoric, and contains appeals to all three of Aristotle's proofs: ethos, logos, and pathos. It follows the classic pattern for speeches and contains all six parts of that pattern: exordium (introduction); narration (statement of facts), proposition (what is to be proven), proofs (appeals to authority), and peroration (closing).

In this section, let's look at Paul's introduction. It is found in verses 1–3: "Brethren, my heart's desire and prayer to God for Israel is, that they might be saved. For I bear them record that they have a zeal of God, but not according to knowledge. For they being ignorant of God's righteousness, and going about to establish their own righteousness, have not submitted themselves unto the righteousness of God."

In this introduction, Paul fulfills all three of the purposes of an introduction. He gets their attention with some provocative words about the Jews. In essence, he is saying that while Israel has a godly zeal, they are also ignorant, self-righteous, and rebellious (a word to the wise: this is Paul . . . *you* are not Paul). At the same time, Paul secures their favor with these words: "Brethren, my heart's desire and prayer to God for Israel is, that they might be saved." He presents himself as having to say some harsh things, but he is not against Israel, certainly doesn't wish them ill; he prays for them and, if he had his way, they would all be saved. In other words, he is saying, "You can trust me to tell you the truth because I have no motive to hurt or punish Israel."

He leads them by using this striking language, and by immediately moving them to his next statement which is essentially his theme, or purpose statement. It is the heart of the truth he wants to communicate: "For Christ is the end of the law for righteousness to everyone that believeth. For Moses describeth the righteousness which is of the law, That the man which doeth those things shall live by them. But the righteousness which is of faith speaketh on this wise, Say not in thine heart, Who shall ascend into heaven? (that is, to bring Christ down from above:) Or, Who shall descend into the deep? (that is, to bring up Christ again from the dead.)" (Romans 10:4–7). This is his transition from the introduction to the body of the sermon; he is asserting that the Law was completed or fulfilled in Jesus and no longer saves people, because its righteousness is based on the works of those who follow it. But faith's righteousness comes by unquestioning belief in Jesus' death, burial, and resurrection. This is why Israel is lost: they continue to trust in the righteousness of the law and question the righteousness of faith and obedience to the gospel.

Methods of Introduction

There are many different ways you can introduce a sermon. Let's look at a few of them. The most common way is usually called the *Textual Method*. It means that your opening sentence is simple and straightforward: "My text this morning is . . . ," then you read your Scripture text. This verse or passage should, of course, be the primary one from which you draw your sermon, or at least the most prominent verse that touches on your theme. The great advantage of this method is that it helps put your audience at ease. It does this because it is familiar to them, since most sermons begin this way; and it assures them you are going to preach from the Bible, which also is reassuring to them. Perhaps most importantly, it helps you be more at ease, since you begin by reading, word for word, something with which you are familiar. This is a great help to calm the jitters. Remember though, this makes the reading of your text part of your introduction. You cannot think of it as a preliminary act that happens before the introduction begins; it is part of the introduction, and because of this, you must read the text with emphasis and emotion. Not overly dramatic, but read with real interest, using inflection in your voice to draw out the meaning of the passage. Sometimes, I will even inject short explanations or asides as I read it, helping to make the text more understandable, especially if those particular nuances will not be used in the sermon. Usually the reading of the text will be followed with telling the story of the text. If it is an event, set the stage: who is involved, where, when, and why. If it is more of a doctrinal or theological passage, discuss who wrote it, to whom, and why. Sometimes after reading the text, you don't discuss the text immediately; instead you utilize another type of introduction altogether. In fact, opening by reading a text will work with all the other methods we will talk about.

Another type of introduction is to *begin with an illustration*. This is extremely effective assuming the illustration is almost perfectly fitted to your purpose statement. If you have to tell it, then explain what you meant by it, don't use it; it won't work. An illustration that does fit, however, is a beautiful thing. The effectiveness of an illustration is governed by several factors, each of which are vital. Remember, *how* you tell a story is more important than the story itself. Stories should be told using concrete nouns and active verbs. The effect of this is a sense of immediacy and a sense of *action*. You don't just want to tell your congregation what happened, you want to take them to the scene and *show* them what happened. That's what a sense of immediacy does: it makes the audience feel like the events of your story are happening *now*. Active verbs *show* them what is happening instead of just telling them. Here is part of one of my favorite sermon introductions. It blends textual exposition (our first type of introduction) with an introduction using an illustration. Its uniqueness is that it uses a little imagination to turn a biblical story into a powerful illustration. As you read it, notice the sense of immediacy and the sense of action. The sermon is "The Woman of the Shattered Romances" by Clovis Chappell:

> Look, will you, at this picture. There sits a man in the strength and buoyancy of young manhood. He is only thirty or thereabouts. About him is the atmosphere of vigor and vitality that belong to the springtime of life. But to-day he is a bit tired. There is a droop in his shoulders. His feet and sandals are dusty. His garment is travel stained. He has been journeying all the morning on foot. And now at the noon hour he is resting.
>
> The place of his resting is an old well curb. The well is one that was digged by hands that have been dust long centuries. This traveler is very thirsty. But he has no means of drawing the water, so he sits upon the well curb and waits. His friends who are journeying with him have gone into the city to buy food. Soon they will return and then they will eat and drink together.

> As he looks along the road that leads into the city he sees somebody coming. That somebody is not one of his disciples. It is a woman. As she comes closer he sees that she is clad in the cheap and soiled finery of her class. At once he knows her for what she is. He reads the dark story of her sinful life. He understands the whole fetid and filthy past through which she has journeyed as through the stenchful mud of a swamp.

Notice the nouns: picture, man, strength, buoyancy, vigor, vitality, springtime, shoulders, feet, sandals, garment, well, curb, hands, water, food, friends, woman, finery, story, life, mud, swamp. All concrete, not an abstract among them. Now the verbs: Look, sits, is, belong, journeying, resting, digged, drawing, waits, gone, buy, return, eat, drink, looks, sees, coming, comes, knows, reads, understands, journeyed. Action everywhere! Even the adverbs and adjectives are robust and colorful. The language puts you there and makes the scene come to life.

An effective illustration introduction can also come from using an understated story that in itself seems not to be connected to the grand theme, but, as becomes apparent, tells the story in miniature, using as much detail as possible to build realism. While more complex and risky, using such an illustration can be as effective in capturing attention as using its more dramatic cousins. This example doesn't come from a sermon, but from one of the most significant books of the twentieth century, if for no other reason than it tells the story of an event that changed the world as few have done. John Hersey begins *Hiroshima* like this:

> At exactly fifteen minutes past eight in the morning, on August 6, 1945, Japanese time, at the moment when the atomic bomb flashed above Hiroshima, Miss Toshiko Sasaki, a clerk in the personnel department of the East Asia Tin Works, had just sat down at her place in the plant office and was turning her head to speak to the girl at the next desk. At that same moment, Dr. Masakazu Fujii was settling down cross-legged to read the Osaka Asahi on the porch of his private hospital, overhanging one of the seven deltaic rivers which divide Hiroshima; Mrs. Hatsuyo Nakamura, a tailor's widow, stood by the window of her kitchen, watching a neighbor tearing down his house because it lay in the path of an air-raid-defense fire lane; Father Wilhelm Kleinsorge, a German priest of the Society of Jesus, reclined in his underwear on a cot on the top floor of his order's three-story mission house, reading a Jesuit magazine, Stimmen der Zeit; Dr. Terufumi Sasaki, a young member of the surgical staff of the city's large, modern Red Cross Hospital, walked along one of the hospital corridors with a blood specimen for a Wassermann test in his hand; and the Reverend Mr. Kiyoshi Tanimoto, pastor of the Hiroshima Methodist Church, paused at the door of a rich man's house in Koi, the city's western

> suburb, and prepared to unload a handcart full of things he had evacuated from town in fear of the massive B-29 raid which everyone expected Hiroshima to suffer. A hundred thousand people were killed by the atomic bomb, and these six were among the survivors.

Hersey uses six mini-stories, one after the other, to draw us in and move us toward the dramatic final line that cannot fail to get our attention and propel us onward into the story: "A hundred thousand people were killed by the atomic bomb, and these six were among the survivors." It makes us think, *how?* and *why?* and *how many others?* But most of all it makes us think *tell me more!* Open a sermon with an introduction that does that, and you will be on your way.

A sort of subgenre to beginning with an illustration is a type sometimes called *a Life Situation* introduction. This type of illustration describes a situation that someone has faced in contemporary life. The idea is to relate a story in which someone has dealt with a dramatic event in life, then to apply his or her way of coping in a more general way so everyone can relate to the story. Of course, it also must illustrate and transition into your theme. Here is an incident from my life that I have used to introduce a sermon titled "Knowing Where to Run."

> I remember the incident very well. It is one of those things that I suppose lodge in your mind when you are a child. One morning my brother

and I were with my dad in an old, black, beat-up pickup truck driving down a dirt road out in a small oil field just outside Kerman, California. Dad pulled to the side of the road and stopped. "Look over there," he said and pointed. It was obviously a place where some horrible accident had happened. As Dad began to explain it to us, we understood what a terrible thing it had been. An oil drilling rig had been operating there the day before. The ruin of it rose from the flat terrain about a hundred yards from us, the top half of the rig lying along the ground, a mass of twisted metal. It was easy, even for us, to realize what had happened; the top of the structure had simply toppled over, crashing onto the rest of it.

As we sat there in the old truck, my dad began to tell us about the driller. Just that morning, leaving for work, Dad said, the driller had told his wife of his concerns about the condition of the rig: "That thing is a piece of junk," he had said. "Somebody's going to get killed one of these days." An accident, I guess, was inevitable. When those pins sheared and the top half of that rig began to fall, the crew began to run. Everybody got off safe, except the driller. He had, from where he was standing on the "floor" when the top began to fall toward him, only two choices of escape routes: He could run to his left and down some stairs and off the rig to safety or he could run to his right across the floor and there, moving quickly behind the huge engine that powered the rig, might find a place of shelter. He had only a split second to decide. Unfortunately, he chose wrong. Running across the floor, he veered right, heading for the safety of the massive engine, but before he could get there, those falling tons of steel pinned him against the radiator and crushed out his life.

Of course, I did not see the body, but my dad had seen it the day before; his face was a study in horror as he turned the tragic incident into an object lesson—a life lesson for his sons. I will never forget the look in my dad's eyes, or the words he spoke to us that day as he described what had happened to the man who ran the wrong way. He said to us: "Always look around you, pay attention, and think ahead. *Always know where to run.* It just might save your life."

Sometimes it is best to begin with a simple, straightforward *statement of your purpose*. It should be brief and direct: "Today I will show scripturally why the baptism of the Holy Ghost is absolutely essential to salvation," or "I'm here to challenge your faith to enable you to see God as willing and able, in fact, eager, to answer your prayers!" Use your purpose statement, just modify it to make it speak directly to your hearers.

The last type I will mention is the *dramatic statement*. The idea is not to woo their attention, seduce them from their distractions, or gently plead for their time; it is to set off a stick of dynamite, turn on a siren, fire up a searchlight. It is to grab them by the nape of the neck and *make* them want to listen. How's that for a dramatic statement? Here are some better examples: in introducing a sermon entitled "What Christ Does for the Soul," Arthur John Gossip makes this dramatic opening:

> What, exactly, has Christ done for you? What is there in your life that needs Christ to explain it, and that, apart from Him, simply could not have been there at all? If there is nothing, then your religion is a sheer futility.

V. A. Guidroz, a master Pentecostal preacher, used this introduction for his often-requested sermon, "The Death March":

> This is a congregation of religious people. We are facing the great catastrophes of the culmination of time. You can't get yourself out of it. You're in it with all your might. You're going to give account of everything that is said in this camp meeting. You can play with it or you can spit it out and walk away from it. But you've got to face it just the same.
>
> We've got to be serious about it. God lives or He's dead. Jesus Christ was the Son of God, born of the virgin Mary or it's the biggest joke in the world. Men and women speak in tongues as inspired by the Holy Ghost or that is the biggest

farce ever put between two lids of a book. Either people are born again or we are just deceiving a whole lot of folks. We have our names written in the Lamb's Book of Life, or we're just playing the biggest joke upon the biggest bunch of innocent people the world has ever known. We either have a Hell beneath us and a Heaven above us, and we've got to win one and lose the other one, or else we are sitting here tonight just playing away our time.

Remember, *dramatic* statement doesn't necessarily mean *provocative* statement, as Paul's was in Romans 10, Gossip's in "What Christ Does for the Soul," or V. A. Guidroz's in "The Death March." Sometimes it catches attention by its striking imagery. F. W. Boreham introduces a sermon (or an essay, sometimes it's hard to tell with Boreham) about delivering bad news called "Breaking the News" like this:

As a general rule, things that are broken are broken by the clumsy. When eggs are broken, or when dishes are broken, or when promises are broken, it is because someone has blundered. But to this general rule there is one striking exception. Careless people may break our china; careless people may break our hearts; but, when it comes to breaking the news, careless people would be worse than useless.

Sometimes, the drama comes from suspense which promises future interesting revelations that pull us into the sermon in spite of ourselves. Boreham uses this technique in "A Tangled Skein," skillfully building the suspense in a brilliant introduction:

> My fingers have often itched to set down the story of Mary Creighton, just as she told it to me that day under the apple-tree, but, until now, my pen has been chained. A newspaper that came last week, however, contains announcements which have effectually brushed away the scruples that I cherished.
>
> Mary Creighton was not her real name: her real name was much prettier, or she made it seem so to me. None of the names that I shall mention are real names. Mary herself was, for years, an inscrutable mystery to me. She was to everybody. Indeed, until that lovely afternoon she made her great confession, I never understood her and I never met anybody who did. A very general feeling prevailed in Mosgiel that, away back in the unforgotten years of Mary's life, a tragedy was buried somewhere; but nobody knew its nature. Innumerable guesses were made: but they were all contradictory, and, therefore, unsatisfactory. No theory squared with *all* the facts. And so it came to pass that the little township gave it up. Mary came to be regarded as a riddle that everybody had asked, but of which nobody knew the answer.

Don't overdo the drama, make it outlandish, or resort to gimmicks. You will get their attention, but they may laugh at you in the process. Years ago when I was a young pastor, I took the advice of a friend and tried a bit of drama to introduce a sermon. The text was from I Corinthians 13:12. "For now we see through a glass, darkly; but then face to face: now I know in part; but then shall I know even as also I am known." After reading this text I had everyone pray, and as they did, I put on a pair of sunglasses I had placed in the pulpit. The idea was to preach about how in the present we are forced to see life through dark glasses, but one day we will take them off and see things as they really are and understand the reasons why life is like it is. The title was "When I Take My Sun Shades Off." It would have been great except for the roar of laughter when the congregation opened their eyes after the prayer and saw me with my shades on. It was so out of character for me that some of my dear saints giggled through the whole sermon. I am still embarrassed as I type these words.

Keep the introduction short; it should do its job and get out of the way. The introduction should not use your best or most powerful material. Of course you must use good stuff in the introduction because of its crucial role, but I have heard preachers who had powerful introductions, but not much else, and things went rapidly downhill. I have even been that preacher on occasion. If all you have is a powerful introduction, wait until you have a powerful sermon to go with it before you use it.

One last comment on introductions. Many great preachers fully write out their introductions, although they may outline the body and the closing. This is a testament to their understanding of just how important introductions are. They know if the introduction suffers from a stall, a misstatement, or a brain freeze, they will spend the rest of the sermon trying to recover. If you fail to capture the audience's attention, arouse their interest, and secure their favor in the introduction, the rest of the sermon is lost. If you are a beginning preacher, write out your introductions. Later, as you gain experience, you may decide you only need detailed notes for the introduction. But by then, who knows? You may be hooked and want to continue to write them out.

The Title

Throughout the process of building your sermon, you should be thinking about the title. There is no real hurry, as the title may come to you at the beginning, in the middle, or at the end of the process. Sometimes the title is easy to come by as the sermon seems to title itself. It was that way with a sermon I titled "Amnon Had a Friend." The text was from II Samuel 13, and in verse 3 we find the pivotal statement of the whole story of Amnon: "But Amnon had a friend." What else could you call that sermon? Usually though, it isn't so easy to find that perfect title. Sometimes, when struggling to come up with the right title, we convince ourselves that the titles don't really matter. "Just name it something," we say, or worse yet, we decide to skip it altogether. But as Rick Warren wrote in *The Art and Craft of Biblical Preaching*,

Writing a great sermon title is an art we must continually work on. I don't know anyone who has mastered it. We all have our hits and misses. But if the purpose of preaching is to transform, not merely inform, or if you're speaking to unbelievers, then you must be concerned with your titles. Like the cover of a book or the first line of an advertisement, your sermon's title must capture the attention of those you want to influence.

The title should contain the promise of the sermon, simply stated. For a sermon that focused on what God can do with nothing (for example, create a universe), and therefore concluded that the less there is of me (that is, the less of my ego, my ambition, and my desire) to get in the way, the more God can do with me, I chose the title, "The Incredible Potential of Nothing." In another sermon I point out that while God is all-powerful and can do anything, there *are* things He cannot do: He cannot fail, make a mistake, lie, or be unjust. The sermon title I chose was "The Limitations of God." For a sermon on the destructive power of sin, I used Samson and King Saul as examples of the tragic end of sin. My introduction used an anecdote from the American Civil War of a witness to the ghoulish robbing of slain soldiers still lying on the field on the morning after a battle. The title was "Stripping the Slain."

If we do it right, the title fits so well that, upon reflection, it seems like it was somehow ordained to be the title of that sermon. Consider Jonathan Edwards's "Sinners in the

Hands of an Angry God." Would anything else have fit that sermon? Charles Spurgeon's "The Stone Rolled Away," Clovis Chappell's "A Good Man's Hell," Stanley Chambers's "Can the United Pentecostal Church Survive the Onslaught of History?" and V. A. Guidroz's "The Death March" are all examples of perfect titles for remarkable sermons.

Avoid being overly cute in your titles. (See "When I Take My Sun Shades Off," above.) A title may be memorable, but for all the wrong reasons, such as giving an impression of immaturity and shallowness. A great sermon doesn't need a cute title. Here are a few overly clever titles taken from church ads in the *Los Angeles Times* and shared by Rick Warren: "Peter Goes Fishing," "The Ministry of Cracked Pots," "Give Me Agape," and "No Such Thing as a Rubber Clock." I am not sure exactly where these titles were meant to go, but I'm pretty sure they didn't get there.

By all means scrutinize your title for unintended meaning. Some borderline suggestive or even vulgar titles have been used by preachers apparently thinking, wrongly, that it would get attention without offending. Maybe they didn't even realize what they were saying. In *Steps to the Sermon*, Brown et al. share a few: "Nudist in a Graveyard" (I assume the demoniac of Gadara.), "The Man Who Wouldn't Leave Women Alone" (I am afraid the preacher may have meant Jesus and the woman at the well, Mary in the garden, the woman taken in adultery, Mary Magdalene, etc.), "The Man, the Woman, and the Hotel Room" (I have no idea), "Why Every Preacher Should Go to Hell" (no comment), and "Kissing in the Dark" (I have tried, but can't think of anything in the Bible this may be referring to). Even if they can be explained by some torturous logic, or tied to some anecdote or illustration, don't ever use such titles.

Here are some questions, suggested by several writers, that you can ask yourself about potential titles to help keep you on track.

Is it arresting? Is it phrased in a way that makes it clear that this sermon has something to say that they will want to hear?

Is it clear? Rick Warren shares a test of this: "If I read this title on a cassette tape five years from today, would I instantly know what the sermon was about?" Substitute "CD" or "file on my computer or phone" for "cassette tape" and you get the idea.

Is it brief? Brown recommends two to seven words, with no more than three or four "strong" words. This is a generalization, of course. A quick look at fifty of my own sermons shows titles which average between three and four words, with a ten-word title the longest and several one-word titles the shortest.

Is it suitable? You are in the house of God, in the pulpit, preaching the Word of God. Act like it.

Is it relevant? The title should make it clear that this will not be a dry, academic discourse. It will be a sermon that addresses your hearers' needs.

The Body of the Sermon

We are making progress: we have our thought, we have written our purpose statement, gathered our materials, begun honing our materials, written our introduction, maybe even settled on our title. Now, we put the sermon together.

The body of the sermon should be made up of three, or sometimes four, or rarely five points that are carefully arranged for the most effective thematic and narrative flow, as well as maximum emotional impact. The points are connected with transitional and explanatory comments. In order to learn to properly order sermon points, we must look at the sermon as a whole, rather than at its parts. A sermon is made up of a title, a text, a first sentence, an introduction, three (and sometimes more) points, and a closing. But each of these must blend with all the others, creating harmony and cohesion that accomplish the purpose of the sermon. Another way of saying this is that they must be arranged so that the sermon *flows* smoothly from the first reading of the text to the final words of the altar appeal toward one goal: to bring people to a place where they will respond to the prompting of the Holy Spirit. Whether that response is to come forward to be baptized in Jesus' name, or to receive the Holy Ghost, or to be healed, or delivered, or blessed; or simply to be closer to God, more willing to obey His word, and thus grow as Christians, the goal of the sermon is the same: to bring them to that point of action. This is done both through the head and the heart, but mostly, for preaching as opposed to teaching, the heart.

It seems to me that there are three considerations you must keep in mind as you craft the body of the sermon: the flow of the theme, the flow of the narrative, and the flow of emotional impact. While each requires different arrangements, and one or the other can be more or less important depending on the sermon, they must be harmonized, fitted together to move the sermon intellectually and emotionally toward its goal. Probably the most flexible, thus the easiest to work with, is narrative flow. You might not think so, since the narrative or *story* of a biblical event happened in a certain order: A happened, then B happened, then C, and finally D. Aren't you pretty well locked into the chronology? Don't you have to tell it the way it happened? Actually, no, you don't. In fact, many times the Bible doesn't either.

Thematic flow is a bit more rigid. It means you have to present your theme in a logical way. Sometimes it is not as much of a need, but often, you must demonstrate the foundational part of your theme, then build on it in successive blocks of truth. It is hard to rearrange this order without befuddling your audience. As a simple example, you may be preaching on humankind's need of God. It might go something like this:

1. Life's greatest tragedy is to be a sinner.
2. "The soul that sinneth" (Ezekiel 18:20).
3. All of us are sinners.
4. "For all have sinned and come short of the glory of God" (Romans 3:23).
5. Because of this, we cannot save ourselves.
6. "It is not in man that walketh to direct his steps" (Jeremiah 10:23).
7. Only God can save us.
8. "For it is not possible that the blood of bulls and of goats" (Hebrews 10:4).

9. He did save us by coming as a man and dying.
10. "Great is the mystery" (I Timothy 3:16).
11. "For God so loved" (John 3:16).
12. Only by obeying the gospel of the death, burial, and resurrection of Jesus can we be saved.
13. "I am the door" (John 10:9).

This is a six-point sermon, but could easily be made into five points by combining points four and five. We can even make it a three-point sermon by making point one part of the introduction, and point six part of the closing. What we cannot easily do is mix up the logical order of the points. The flow of the logic moves from the foundational premise, that being a sinner is a great tragedy, and then proceeds, each point arising out of and resting on the preceding point. All are sinners, we cannot save ourselves. Only God can save, and He has established a way for us to be saved. He did this by coming as Jesus Christ and dying on the cross, rising again, and offering the gift of the Holy Ghost. And we can only be saved by embracing this offer through obeying the gospel. This is the logical flow, and it is difficult to change.

The most important consideration is the flow of the emotional impact of the sermon. It is this that is most vital to bring the hearers to a point of response. Ian Pitt-Watson, writing in *The Art and Craft of Biblical Preaching*, calls this emotive flow the "cardiovascular system" or the "bloodstream" of the sermon. He asserts that until we have *felt* the truth of the gospel, we have not *heard* the full gospel. He goes on:

Preaching involves a kind of passionate thinking. Sometimes the preacher is giving conceptual expression to what the hearer had previously only felt to be true, but at other times the preacher is expressing as a felt truth something the hearer had previously only thought to be true. Both tasks are equally important, and for both a healthy cardiovascular system is required that can express felt truths and carry the affect (the feel) of these truths to every limb and organ of the sermon. This is the lifeblood of preaching.

Every Scripture, every story, every illustration has an emotional effect, some greater than others. It is essential that you learn to gauge the impact each has, and arrange them within your sermon to provide a flow of emotion, gradually building toward the invitation and the opportunity to respond to the Spirit. When I say "gradually building," I don't mean moving in a straight line from the least impactful to the most impactful. This is hard to do, and not very effective, because an audience doesn't react well to that. Similarly, they do not react well to a sermon that takes off like a rocket, reaches a high level of emotion immediately, and tries to sustain that high level for the duration of the sermon. Emotion must build, and that requires ebbs and flows, moments of high emotion followed by less emotion, then even higher emotion.

Let's further explore this concept visually using the following graphs.

This is an emotionally dead and therefore boring sermon:

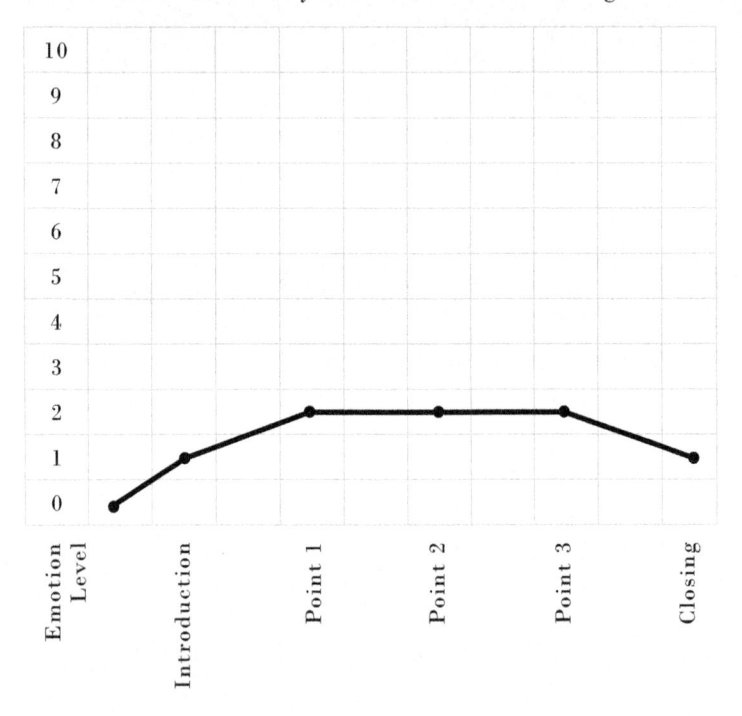

It fails because, though it may be doctrinally sound and intellectually stimulating, it does not engage the heart. At the end, the response will be out of duty or routine, and the time of prayer will likely be short. This is not an effective approach, even for teaching. You should always try to vary the emotional impact of your points in order to hold your congregation's attention.

This is an emotionally exhausting sermon:

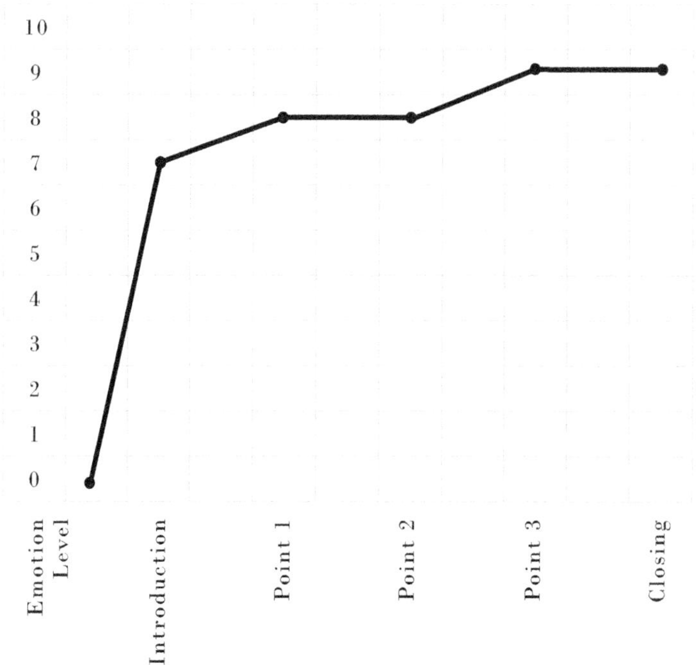
10
9
8
7
6
5
4
3
2
1
0
Emotion Level
Introduction
Point 1
Point 2
Point 3
Closing

This takes people to near the top of their emotional capacity and expects to keep them there. While some can stay with a sermon like this, many can't, it is too exhausting. Unless you plan to speak fifteen minutes or less, or the Holy Spirit has taken over and is driving this, avoid this approach.

This is better than the first two, but still expects too much out of a congregation:

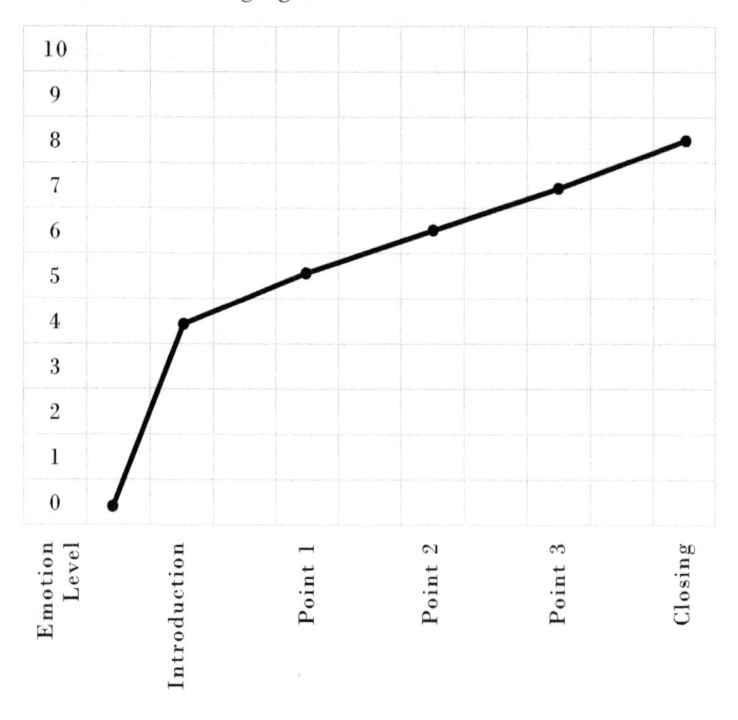

[Chart showing Emotion Level from 0 to 10 across Introduction, Point 1, Point 2, Point 3, Closing. Values rise from 0 to 4 at Introduction, 5 at Point 1, 6 at Point 2, 7 at Point 3, and 8 at Closing.]

Notice, the emotional level never dips; it continues to get higher and higher, with no chance for the audience to catch its breath, to absorb what is being said, and to prepare emotionally for what is coming next.

This is probably the ideal:

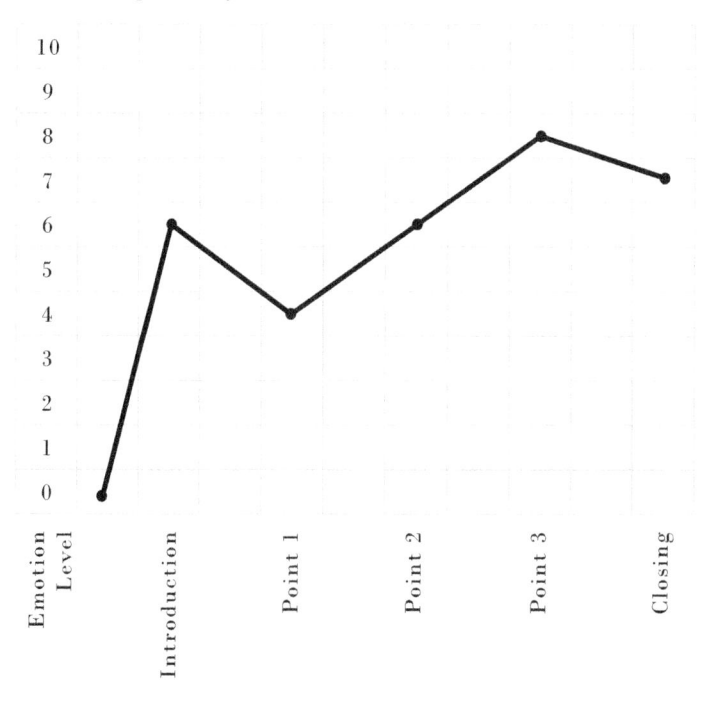

Component	Emotion Level
Introduction	6
Point 1	4
Point 2	6
Point 3	8
Closing	7

The emotional impact of the introduction catches their attention and wakes them up. The first point allows them to settle down, catch their breath, and begin to be touched by the Word. The second point begins the ramp up, and the last point is the most impactful of all, moving them into the emotion of the closing, and into the appeal.

So, by identifying the emotional effect of each component of the sermon, we can arrange the body of the sermon in the most effective way, within the confines of the logic of our argument, to bring our hearers to a point of responding to the voice of the Spirit.

The Closing

Never summarize as an ending to your sermon. A summary is a point by point review of what you have just preached: "So as you can see, when we open our hearts to the gospel, God (1) forgives our sins, (2) transfers them to the cross of Christ by our being baptized in Jesus' name, (3) fills us with His Holy Spirit, and (4) through His Spirit, empowers us to live a holy life." You might as well end with, "Are there any questions?"

The choice of the word *closing* rather than *conclusion* or *summary* is deliberate.

You close a sermon in the same way a salesman closes a deal: you want them to sign on the dotted line. The difference is you are offering the greatest deal ever offered in history: a new beginning, a fresh start, a brand new life in exchange for the old one. Your job is to convince them it isn't too good to be true, it's just true, and available now. There will be more on closing the sermon and making the invitation later.

The Notes

Now it is time to prepare the sermon notes. These notes are what you will take to the pulpit with you. There are many different formats that can be used for these notes. This is probably a matter of personal taste as much as anything else. Some preachers use bullet points, some bold font and italics, some use formal outline rules, others simply write down sentence by sentence or thought by thought without any outlining at all. The only thing to keep in mind is that the material must be almost instantly see-able. You need, while in the pulpit, to be able to easily find your place once it is lost. Learn to create notes that keep what you need to know segmented into the broad outlines of the sermon, before your eyes, so you can find what you need when you need it.

I began outlining my sermons a long time ago and developed the habit of using a formal outline format. I use the traditional style:

I. Major Heading 1
   A. First Point
      1. Subpoint that explains or illuminates first point
         a. Subpoint that explains or illuminates subpoint 1
         b. Subpoint that explains or illuminates subpoint 1
      2. Subpoint that explains or illuminates first point
   B. Second Point
II. Major Heading 2

For me this type of outline is so familiar that I can quickly follow the major points, moving away from the notes and back to them quickly and seamlessly, finding exactly where I need to be. You may find another outline scheme fits better, and that's fine. The point is, find what works for you and use it.

EXAMPLE SERMON

Before we continue putting our sermon together, let's settle on the title. There is no certain time in the process better than any other, so let's do it now. As a refresher, here are the highlights of our section on titles:

The title should contain the promise of the sermon, simply stated.

- Avoid being overly cute in your titles.
- Scrutinize your title for unintended meaning.
- Is the title arresting? Is it clear? Is it brief? Is it suitable? Finally, is it relevant?

To begin, let's go back to our purpose statement to determine the "promise of the sermon." Here it is: "My purpose is to show that even when we aren't sure of what God will do, if we act on whatever faith we have, rather than surrendering to our doubt, God will respond to our need." The promise of the sermon is to encourage those who struggle with doubt by pointing out God will still respond even when our faith is weak. As I think about that, I realize the arresting word in my purpose statement is "doubt," not "faith." We have heard many sermons on faith, but few on doubt; plus, relieving the anxiety almost all of us have about our doubt is the promise of the sermon.

In gathering my materials, I came across a sermon

Putting It All Together

I prepared when I was pastoring in the St. Louis area which is similar to the sermon we are constructing now. It focuses on the fact that, as an answer to a request, a *maybe* is always better than a *no*. I called this sermon "Taking Advantage of a Doubt." I like that sermon and title and will certainly use parts of the sermon, but I think we can do better on the title.

It strikes me that I want to cast this sermon as answering a question; namely, what effect does the presence of doubt have on receiving the miraculous from God? So, why not phrase the title as the question we are answering? We don't want to put too fine a point on it, and the title "What Effect Does the Presence of Doubt Have on Receiving the Miraculous from God?" at fourteen words is too long, so let's simplify and shorten it. At the same time, if we can make it a bit more dramatic, a bit more arresting, let's do that, too. One way is to use rhythm and cadence. This is done by using repetitive words or word sounds. Let's ask ourselves, what rhymes with doubt? Snout . . . lout . . . without . . . about. There you go: "about." Let's use "What About Doubt?" It asks the question we want to answer, it is not overly cute, no unintended meaning, it is arresting, clear, brief, suitable, and relevant. It has a little rhythm, and uses parachesis (the repetition of word sounds). I like it.

Now that we have settled on a title for our sermon, let's settle on the text. Let's use the story of the four lepers: this is our second-most impactful story and I plan to place it last among our points in the body. We could use the story of the father who brought his son to Jesus,

We Preach

which we would normally do since it is the most impactful, but as I mentioned earlier, I have something special in mind for this story, so I don't want to lessen its impact by "giving it away" too soon, which using it as the text would do. So we will read II Kings 7:3–5 as our text:

> And there were four leprous men at the entering in of the gate: and they said one to another, Why sit we here until we die?
> If we say, We will enter into the city, then the famine is in the city, and we shall die there: and if we sit still here, we die also. Now therefore come, and let us fall unto the host of the Syrians: if they save us alive, we shall live; and if they kill us, we shall but die.
> And they rose up in the twilight, to go unto the camp of the Syrians: and when they were come to the uttermost part of the camp of Syria, behold, there was no man there.

We have our text and title, now we will begin constructing the introduction. As you remember, this is a crucial part of the sermon. You must start right, or you will struggle ever after. I have gathered some materials about doubt: why we are so prone to it, why it is such a part of the human experience. My opening paragraphs would go something like this:

> We live in an age of doubt. Our children are taught in school, as we were taught, the scientific method: which is to doubt, to question, everything.

This has led to the undermining of faith as perhaps nothing else in our history. So-called Situation Ethics, the teaching that there is no right or wrong but only the shifting sand of situation, leaves us all in doubt. Does it really matter how I live? Does it matter if I am honest, if I am fair, if I am kind, if I am compassionate? Does anything in human behavior really matter? If lying, stealing, even murder can be justified by the situation, where is solid ground on which I can stand?

The elevating of evolution almost to religious status, the rejection of traditional Christian moral standards, the acceptance of abortion, the mainstreaming of promiscuity and homosexuality as not just acceptable, but celebrated lifestyles, have all undermined belief in the Bible as the Word of God. We have relegated the Bible to a collection of sayings, myths, and outmoded rules. And, since we have cut loose from the Bible, we know nothing about God, not even if He exists. And since we don't know Him, we no longer know ourselves.

Not only is doubt ingrained in modern culture, it is in human nature to doubt. We are locked into our five senses, prisoners of our incomplete understanding. We pray and sometimes are not healed, the miracle does not happen, the loved one does not come to God. No one here has not struggled with doubt. It is our nature.

Today I am not going to try to talk you out of your doubts. I think I could, at least for a while.

I could talk to you about the Bible picture of a caring God:

I Peter 5:7 "Casting all your care upon him; for he careth for you."

Ephesians 3:20 "Now unto him that is able to do exceeding abundantly above all that we ask or think, according to the power that worketh in us."

John 14:14 "If ye shall ask any thing in my name, I will do it."

I could talk to you about the miracles that I have witnessed. (Here you would insert brief accounts of two or three healings, deliverances, or other miraculous events you have witnessed or experienced.)

But I believe, even if I could talk you out of your doubts, they would come back tomorrow, or the next day, perch on your shoulder, and whisper in your ear: "I believe He did it for them, but He won't do it for you. He did it then, but not now. He did it there but not here."

So here's what I am going to do. I am going to urge you to act upon your doubts. Even if you are not sure there is a God; if in your mind He is only a maybe, then act on that maybe. If, in your mind the blessings of God are only a possibility, then act on that possibility. If in your thinking you have only a slim chance of being saved, then act on that chance. I am preaching on the premise that a doubtful step *toward* God is better than the most certain step *away* from Him.

I like it! But we could make it better. I think I would get rid of the first two paragraphs. They are good, and I will certainly save them for the future, but they may be a distraction here. Your introduction should be razor sharp with as few competing thoughts as possible: you don't want your hearers' minds reeling as they try to process several striking ideas at once. Besides, I don't want to blame somebody else for our proclivity to doubt, I want to keep the focus where it belongs: on us.

So skipping the social commentary, I move immediately to our own tendency to doubt. Since I have eliminated two paragraphs, I have the time to punch up paragraph three, make it clearer, better. I begin my introduction like this:

> It is human nature to doubt. We are locked into our five senses, prisoners of our incomplete understanding; and because we know there is so much we do not see, so much we do not hear, we come to doubt what we know, and we become less sure. Our experiences too, rob our confidence: we pray and sometimes are not healed, the miracle does not happen, the loved one does not come to God. There is no one here who is so spiritual that they have not struggled with doubt. It is our nature to doubt . . .

There are two other things I want to do to my introduction. First, I want to include the question we are planning to answer: What effect does the presence of doubt have on receiving the miraculous from God? Second, I want to punch up the impact of the introduction. It already has a lot, but can do with more. What are its emotional highpoints, so far? The first is the statement, "No one here is so spiritual that they have not struggled with doubt." This has impact because it is true, but seldom talked about. It also creates a sense of togetherness. It will cause some hearers to think, "I am not alone." Some will shake their heads yes, and make eye contact with others in the room. This statement will pull them into the sermon. The second is the powerful statement that hints at the answer to our question: "I am preaching on the premise that a doubtful step *toward* God is better than the most certain step *away* from Him." Give this a moment to sink in; you will like the result.

Now, we will raise the emotional impact even more by introducing the demon-possessed child and his desperate father. Almost always, you save the most impactful point of a sermon to use as the final point. Why, then, use the father and the demon-possessed son in the introduction rather than later? There's a couple of reasons. One is because of a striking text within that story that underlines and effectively introduces the theme of the sermon. That text is the honest cry of the father: "I believe, help Thou my unbelief!" This admission of the reality that faith is often (if not usually) mixed with doubt not only describes our own reality when it comes to faith and doubt, but perfectly sets up our sermon. Second, this story also includes a Scripture verse that we had already identified as emphasizing the role of faith in the miraculous. This verse is Mark 9:23: "Jesus said unto him, 'If thou canst believe, all things are possible to him that believeth.'" We do not want to leave the impression that we are preaching that faith is not important, an obviously unscriptural position, so better to make that clear early on in the message. This text will do it. Finally, the story can easily be split into two parts, lessening its initial impact, but enhancing its later emotional effect. We will quickly describe the story of the father appealing to Jesus after the disciples had failed to help him: Jesus tells him in no uncertain terms that his miracle is dependent on his faith, and he answers with his description of his faith/doubt mixture, and we stop there, pointing out that we are like the father more often than not. Later, at the beginning of our closing, we will point out that Jesus was not offended by the presence of doubt, nor the honest admission of it: indeed, the boy was healed in spite of the father's doubt. He will do the same for us. The power of splitting the story is that the body of the sermon will pile evidence upon evidence that God responds to even the weakest of faith, in the face of doubt itself, until the truth of it is inescapable. Then, after all that evidence, the hearer is brought back to the very first story they heard, the story they immediately identified with: "Yeah, I *am* like that father!" and shows that this story too, is proof that God chooses to respond to our faith and ignore our doubt.

So, putting this together we craft our title, text, and introduction:

What About Doubt?
II Kings 7:3–5

"And there were four leprous men at the entering in of the gate: and they said one to another, Why sit we here until we die?

If we say, We will enter into the city, then the famine is in the city, and we shall die there: and if we sit still here, we die also. Now therefore come, and let us fall unto the host of the Syrians: if they save us alive, we shall live; and if they kill us, we shall but die.

And they rose up in the twilight, to go unto the camp of the Syrians: and when they were come to the uttermost part of the camp of Syria, behold, there was no man there."

I. Introduction

It is human nature to doubt. We are locked into our five senses, prisoners of our incomplete understanding; and because we know there is so much we do not see, so much we do not hear, we come to doubt what we know, and we become less sure. Our experiences too, rob us of our confidence: we pray and sometimes are not healed, the miracle does not happen, the loved one does not come to God. There is no one here who is so spiritual that they have not struggled with doubt. It is our nature to doubt.

In fact, if we are honest, we are, more often than not, like the father who brought his son to Jesus for healing in Mark 9. A demon possessed the boy, throwing him into the fire, and into water, trying to destroy the child. The disciples of Jesus had been unable to help, and now, desperate, the father comes to Jesus Himself, the Master is his last hope. He relates the story of his son's torment, and Jesus says to him, "If thou canst believe, all things are possible to him that believeth." I don't want you to misunderstand what I am saying in this sermon: faith is the coin of the realm of Heaven, it takes faith to receive from God; in fact, without faith it is impossible to please God. But let's be honest, as this father was when Jesus reminded him of the necessity of faith, the Bible says: And straightway the father of the child cried out, and said with tears, "Lord, I believe; help thou mine unbelief." That is us! Seldom do we have that certain faith that banishes all doubt. Most often, like that father, we believe enough to ask God for help, but doubt lurks in our heart, wondering if He will help us.

We need to settle the question, what about doubt? Does doubt disqualify us from receiving from God?

In this sermon, I am not going to try to talk you out of your doubts. I think I could, at least for a while. I could talk to you about the Bible picture of a caring God:

I Peter 5:7 "Casting all your care upon him; for he careth for you."

Ephesians 3:20 "Now unto him that is able to

do exceeding abundantly above all that we ask or think, according to the power that worketh in us."

John 14:14 "If ye shall ask any thing in my name, I will do it."

I could talk to you about the miracles that I have witnessed. In my own family, just a little over a year ago we saw the miraculous. My wife went to her doctor for some routine imaging, no problems, just time to do it. Within a few days she got a postcard, then a phone call: "Mrs. Jones, please make an appointment at the hospital for some further testing, we have found something we are concerned about." They told her of a mass they had detected, the size of it, the exact location of it. I confess, God and I had a heart to heart. We were afraid, knowing what this could mean, and it was reflected in our prayers. Mine was, "God, I ain't having it! You said you would never put more on us than we could bear. Well, we can't bear this!" I admit, my faith was not so strong.

I will never forget dropping off my wife at the hospital door, parking the car, and walking through a cold rain to join her, or sitting with my wife in the waiting room for what seemed like hours. Then when she was called to the back, it seemed like a century passed, before she emerged, smiling. "Let's go into the hall," she said, and I followed her. When we got into the hallway, she said, "Well, they did all the things they needed to do, and then told me, 'Mrs. Jones, go home and forget about it, whatever was there, simply isn't there anymore!'" Our God is a miracle-worker! He will heal, save, deliver; and He will do it for you!

But I believe, even if I could talk you out of your doubts, they would come back tomorrow, or the next day, and perch on your shoulder, and whisper in your ear: "I believe He did it for them, but He won't do it for you. He did it then, but not now. He did it there but not here."

So what I am going to do, I am going to urge you to act upon your doubts. Even if you are not sure there is a God; if in your mind He is only a maybe, then act on that maybe. If in your mind the blessings of God are only a possibility, then act on that possibility. If in your thinking you have only a slim chance of being saved, then act on that chance. I am preaching on the premise that a doubtful step toward God is better than the most certain step away from Him.

The Bible is full of examples of this truth; in fact, the challenge was not to find illustrations, it was to choose among the many. What about Esther?

Now, on to the development of the body. After the introduction has gotten their attention, you should insert the three points in the order of their emotional effect. I feel that order would be Esther, Nineveh, and the four lepers. We will outline our points. Certainly if you want to write the entire sermon word for word, go for it. The body will look like this:

II. Esther
   A. Haman's plot to destroy Mordecai and all the Jews
   B. Mordecai sends Esther word: You must go before the king.
   C. Esther sends word back:
      1. I don't know; it is illegal to enter the throne room uninvited.
      2. If the king doesn't like it, I could be put to death.
   D. Mordecai answers: if you do nothing two things are certain.
      1. All Jews will die.
      2. You are a Jew.
      3. If you go to the king you *may* die, if you don't you *will* die.
   E. Esther's response: "I go in unto the king, which is not according to the law: and if I perish, I perish."
   F. She went in, and the king was not angry.
      1. He lifted his golden scepter.
      2. "Whatever you want, up to half the kingdom!"
   G. Our King awaits us. Maybe you aren't sure but come to Him anyway!
III. Nineveh
   A. "Yet forty days, and Nineveh shall be overthrown!"
      1. Jonah did not care. In fact, he wanted them to be punished.

2. There is no record they heard from their preacher any hope at all.
   a. Never mentioned repentance
   b. Never mentioned mercy
B. They acted on their doubt: Jonah 3:6–9 "For word came unto the king of Nineveh, and he arose from his throne, and he laid his robe from him, and covered him with sackcloth, and sat in ashes. And he caused it to be proclaimed and published through Nineveh by the decree of the king and his nobles, saying, Let neither man nor beast, herd nor flock, taste any thing: let them not feed, nor drink water: But let man and beast be covered with sackcloth, and cry mightily unto God: yea, let them turn every one from his evil way, and from the violence that is in their hands. *Who can tell if God will turn and repent, and turn away from his fierce anger, that we perish not?*"
   1. Jonah built his church with a seating capacity of one, and waited for judgment.
   2. But God heard their repentance, even though they were not sure He would.

IV. The Lepers
A. I have always been impressed with the logic of these men.
   1. Trapped between the besieged, dying city of Samaria, and the ruthless, merciless Syrians, they reviewed their choices.
   2. They only knew two things that were certain.

            a. If we go into the city, we will die.
            b. If we stay here in the gate, we will also die.
        3. Only one thing that was uncertain
            a. If we go to the Syrians they may kill us.
            b. *Or* they may not kill us.
    B. They chose the only real hope, though they were doubtful of the outcome.
        1. They "rose in the twilight to go to the Syrian camp."
        2. When they got there, the Syrians were gone.
    C. This is how four starving lepers ate king's food, dressed in king's robes, and delivered a dying city.

Now we want to put our closing together. The emotion will be high at the end of the story of the lepers. People are beginning to see the point, and for many it will be a revelation. They will be ready to bring their faith to God, trusting the truth you have just preached that their doubt does not disqualify them from receiving from God. Because of this, the closing should not be long, but it should maintain the impact of the body of the sermon, and get people to respond.

Here's what I would do:

V. Closing
    A. God is not insulted when we come to Him uncertain, even doubtful.

1. When that desperate father cried out, I believe, help thou my unbelief
   a. Jesus did not send him away.
   b. Jesus did not say "I can't help you."
   c. What He did was set that boy free, answer that father's prayer.
   d. He will do the same for you!
2. When that leper came timidly to Jesus and called to Him: "Lord, if thou wilt, thou canst make me clean."
   a. What he was saying is, "I believe You *can*, but I don't know if You *will*."
   b. Jesus was not insulted, turned off, angered.
   c. What He did was "put forth his hand, and touched him, saying, I will; be thou clean. And immediately his leprosy was cleansed."
3. When the prodigal son woke up at the hog pen he decided to go home.
   a. He did not know the reception he would receive.
   b. "I'm not worthy to be your son."
   c. "I'll live with the servants."
   d. But the Father ran to meet him, and welcomed him home.

B. Why don't you come to Him?
   1. He is coming to meet you.
   2. Don't let doubt rob you of what God wants to do for you. Come now.

> One final comment. In this closing, detail is not your friend; don't slow down to set any scenes, explain who any of these characters are, how they got in their predicaments, or what their thought processes are. If the audience suspects you have three more points, they may tune you out. Create the scenes with only a few words, but use powerful ones, and move quickly to the prodigal and his father in the road, and then give the altar call.

Sources Cited in Chapter 9

Roger Ailes and Jon Kraushar, *You Are the Message: Secrets of the Master Communicators* (New York: Bantam Doubleday Dell, 1989).

Donald E. Demaray, *An Introduction to Homiletics* (Grand Rapids: Baker, 1974).

Clovis Chappell, "The Woman of the Shattered Romances," in *Sermons on Biblical Characters* (Garden City, NY: Doubleday Doran, 1928).

John Hersey, *Hiroshima* (New York: Alfred A. Knopf, 1946).

Jerry Jones, "Knowing Where to Run," in *Amnon Had a Friend and Other Sermons* (Hazelwood, MO: Word Aflame, 2006).

Arthur John Gossip, "What Christ Does for a Soul," in *From the Edge of the Crowd* (Edinburgh: T.&T. Clark, 1924).

V. A. Guidroz, "The Death March" a description of the sermon and the introduction can be found at https://www.pentecostalherald.com/articles/article/old-sermons-still-live-preaching-vily-able-guidroz.

F. W. Boreham, "Breaking the News" and "A Tangled Skein" in *Wisps of Wildfire* (London: Epworth Press, 1924).

Rick Warren, "The Purpose-Driven Title," in Haddon Robinson and Craig Brian Larson, eds., *The Art and Craft of Biblical Preaching* (Grand Rapids: Zondervan, 2005).

Jonathan Edwards, "Sinners in the Hands of an Angry God" is available from several online sources. I referenced http://www.jonathan-edwards.org/Sinners.html.

Charles H. Spurgeon, "The Stone Rolled Away," in *Twelve Sermons on the Resurrection* (Grand Rapids: Baker, 1968).

Clovis Chappell, "A Good Man's Hell," in *Sermons On Biblical Characters* (Garden City, NY: Doubleday Doran, 1928).

Stanley Chambers, "Can the United Pentecostal Church Survive the Onslaught of History?" was preached at the General Conference of the United Pentecostal Church International in 1967.

Ian Pitt-Watson, "Lifeblood of Preaching," in Haddon Robinson and Craig Brian Larson, eds., *The Art and Craft of Biblical Preaching* (Grand Rapids: Zondervan, 2005).

Part Four

In the Pulpit: Presentation

> The orator persuades by means of his hearers, when they are roused to emotion by his speech; for the judgments we deliver are not the same when we are influenced by joy or sorrow, love or hate.
>
> Aristotle

Come to that very field of preaching, that of public speaking. Recall the truly appalling urgency which rested on Mr. Winston Churchill in June 1940. An imminent invasion, the issue of which no one knew but all could fear, placed upon him the necessity of playing the role of an Atlas, of getting under a whole nation and literally lifting it up to a new level of fortitude and faith and the will to endure.... [T]o a large degree Mr. Churchill could bring what the urgency of the crisis demanded—the superb technique of a man who had worked for a lifetime with words. The Nazis had talked much of secret weapons, but England had two secret weapons which the Nazis did not know. One was Gibbon. The other was Macaulay. Mr. Churchill had learned a craftsman's way with words and sentences from both of them. When he was a young army officer in India, he gave long hours to both of these favorite authors. They helped to give a rhythm to his speech which in a real way matched the rhythm of the pulse in men's bodies.... When the British came to "their finest hour," they responded to a technique adequate to the urgency. Anyone could have shouted, "Let us be brave." It was the artist who could etch an unforgettable picture in the minds of millions, the picture of a defending army giving ground but never giving up: "We shall defend our island, whatever the cost may be, we shall fight on the landing grounds, we shall fight in the fields and in the streets, we shall fight in the hills; we shall never surrender." It was the artist who lifted a nation to its feet.

Halford E. Luccock

In the Pulpit: Presentation

You have dedicated your life to God, you have given yourself to study, you have sought for direction, found a "thought," studied your Scripture passage, gathered your materials, chosen your illustrations, gauged the impact of each point, prepared your notes. Now, it is time to preach.

10

GETTING AND KEEPING ATTENTION

> I have devoted my life to answer one question: Why is it that some can preach for an hour and it seems like five minutes while others preach for only five minutes and it seems like an hour?
>
> Haddon Robinson

> Indeed the orator is the embodiment of the passions of the multitude. Before he can inspire them with any emotion he must be swayed by it himself. When he would rouse their indignation his heart is filled with anger. Before he can move their tears his own must flow. To convince them he must himself believe.
>
> Winston Churchill

In the last chapter of this book, I will discuss the role of the anointing in the pulpit. I hope you will read it carefully and prayerfully. Without the anointing, preaching is mere public speaking, and even the best public speaking, though it can inspire its hearers to action, lacks the supernatural power needed to transform people's lives. Always, always seek the anointing.

But it is also true that the anointing can be hindered by poor preparation and poor presentation. Hopefully, the last three chapters have helped insure you are well prepared when you step to the pulpit. But no matter how firmly based on the Bible, how well-structured, and how well-illustrated, if your sermon is not presented in an effective way, it will fail to accomplish all that it should. There are skills that can be learned that will capture your congregation's attention and keep them engaged with your sermon, opening their hearts to the supernatural. The lack of these skills can hinder the work of the Word and the Spirit by distracting, or failing to capture the congregation's attention in the first place. In this chapter we will discuss some of those skills.

At the very least your presentation should minimize distractions that will draw the hearer's attention from the sermon. Wildly mispronounced words, exaggerated expressions, clownish gestures, convoluted syntax, repetition of phrases, and inappropriate dress can all get in the way of the message reaching the hearts of its hearers. You have probably heard the stories of young people in the congregation counting the number of times the preacher said "Amen!" or "Hallelujah!" If they are doing that, they are probably not listening to whatever else you are saying.

Show and Tell

First, we will discuss the nonverbal or silent aspects of your presentation. These include mannerisms, facial expressions, and body language. Whether planned and deliberately executed, or coming without thought or even awareness from your subconscious, they can be just as important as the spoken word in effectively preaching a sermon, and so deserve close attention.

Mannerisms are the often-unconscious ways you habitually move, respond, or otherwise behave. They are the idiosyncrasies that make you identifiably you: the way you walk, the certain tilt of your head when you are in deep thought, the way you move your hands when you talk. All of these can be a help in communicating your message or a distraction that takes away from it.

Facial expressions are the emotions, reactions, and silent messages sent to your hearers by the expressions that move across your face as you preach. If your message conveys the need for urgent action, but your face remains placid and unemotional, the effect will be ruined. A fixed smile while preaching about the sufferings of Jesus on the cross or the terrible cost of sin will send conflicting and confusing messages, and your congregation will be unresponsive. The Churchill quote at the beginning of this chapter is true: you must feel the emotions you wish to inspire in those who hear you. But just feeling them is not enough, you must show that you feel them, and the expression on your face is the best way to do this.

Body language is everything from your posture, to your gestures, to whether you are nervous or relaxed, confident or unsure of yourself. Your body language can be a powerful tool to bring stories to life and help capture your congregation's attention; likewise, out-of-sync, wooden, or nervous body language is a deadly distraction.

These three silent communicators are incredibly important if you want to improve your preaching. John Broadus reminds us that, "In many cases a gesture is much more expressive than any number of words." To illustrate, he quotes Herbert Spencer:

> How truly language must be regarded as a hindrance to thought, though the necessary instrument of it, we shall clearly perceive on remembering the comparative force with which simple ideas are communicated by signs. To say, "leave the room," is less expressive than to point to the door. Placing a finger on the lips is more forcible than whispering, "Do not speak." A beck of the hand is better than "Come here." No phrase can convey the idea of surprise so vividly as opening the eyes and raising the eyebrows. A shrug of the shoulders would lose much by translation into words.

When you recognize the power of mannerisms, facial expression, and body language to speak when no words are being said, it is clear that to bring these three methods of pulpit communication together in harmony multiplies the power of each of them. On this, Broadus quotes Robert Louis Dabney:

> He who is master of this sign-language has, indeed, an almost magic power. When the orator can combine it with the spoken language, he acquires thereby exceeding vivacity of expression. Not only his mouth but his eyes, his features, his fingers speak. The hearers read the coming sentiment upon his countenance and limbs almost before his voice reaches their ears: they are both spectators and listeners; every sense is absorbed in charmed attention.

In order to begin to use the silent communicators to your advantage, first you must eliminate the distractions they can cause. Get the video of your last sermon, or if one isn't available, video yourself preaching. Study that video. What you are looking for is not the highlights, but the lowlights (there are always some, and sometimes a lot). Don't get distracted admiring your great sermon. *What* you say isn't important for what we are doing; *how* you say it is what we are after. If you have to, turn the sound down. Watch yourself carefully while trying to imagine the image on the screen is not you. You're looking first for mannerisms: habits, quirks, tics; anything that will distract the audience. Be honest with yourself, could you spend most of an hour watching and listening to this person preach and really hear what he or she has to say? Or would your attention be drawn to something he or she is doing that simply will not let you focus on the sermon?

Next, watch the facial expressions of the person on the screen. Ask yourself, do they look panicked? Stern? Angry?

Scared? Decide what is the one thing above all others conveyed by the face of the preacher on the screen. Write that one thing down, think about it, and ask yourself, is this what I want to communicate to the congregation?

Finally, analyze the body language of the preacher you are watching. Once again decide the impression you receive from the way the preacher moves, gestures, walks, and worships. Is the preacher comfortable in front of the congregation? Are his movements natural, or obviously practiced and forced? Is he stiff, wooden, seemingly afraid to move, unsure of himself? Does the preacher make consistent eye-contact with the audience? Do her eyes move from person to person, across the congregation, not shifty, but meeting their eyes, inviting them as individuals to listen?

If you are courageous enough, and self-confident enough, ask someone you trust to watch the same video and go through the same process: look first for distracting mannerisms, next facial expressions, and finally, body language. Ask them to record their impressions and share them with you. If you do this, you can't be thin-skinned or defensive. Do not explain, argue, or justify anything, just listen carefully and encourage your critic to be brutally honest. The idea of this exercise is to compare what someone else saw with what you saw in order to help identify potential problems, ultimately to help you be a better preacher. Nothing they see is permanent, nothing they mention means you aren't cut out to be a preacher, nothing will be unique to you. They will all be problems common to nearly all preachers. Don't forget to sincerely thank whoever does it, you owe them big time.

Start working on the main issues you identified by studying the video. When you have overcome the one main problem in each area studied, then do the process all over again, and go to work on the next issue you identify. Remember only the most egregious issues demand frantic, emergency effort. Preaching is a life work; you will never be perfect, just commit yourself to steady improvement.

Powerful Preaching

Never lose sight of the fact that, even though this chapter is titled "Getting and Keeping Attention," the congregation's attention is not, in itself, the ultimate goal. Attention is a means to the real end, and that end is to create an atmosphere, through the preached Word, for the power of God to move, for people to respond, and for them to receive what they need from God. Phillips Brooks lists five characteristics or elements that are the source of power in preaching. All of them except the first have to do with how preachers handle themselves while in the pulpit. They are as follows:

1. Character
2. Freedom from self-consciousness
3. Enjoyment of the work
4. Gravity (Gravitas)
5. Courage

We have already considered the preacher's character at some length in previous chapters, so it should be sufficient here to say you must be real so that you can project genuine sincerity when you walk into the pulpit, and throughout the sermon. It is devastating to the sermon if there is a lack of sincerity because you are not who you pretend to be. You need not be perfect, but you must be real. Let's look at the other four.

Number two is *freedom from self-consciousness*. This is one that doesn't come easy. When you step to the pulpit, you mustn't be thinking of yourself and what people may think of your preaching. This self-absorption leads to nervousness, timidity, and even stage fright. Never preach thinking of how to impress your hearers; that is not your purpose. Don't preach to make a name for yourself, further your career, or get more invitations to preach. Of course, for good or ill, all these things are affected by how well you do in the pulpit, but they are by-products, they are not your purpose. Keep your eye on the ball. If you don't, you are doomed to failure.

How do you banish self-consciousness from your preaching? One way is by focusing on the needs of those who will hear you. As you join in the worship service, scan the congregation, not as a group of people, but as individuals. Look at their faces. See them as hurting, needy human beings who have come to hear from God. Your success is not gauged by how well you do, but how much you help them. Remind yourself that this is what the Word is designed to do, and if preached sincerely it will accomplish its purpose.

Transfer your attention from yourself to your hearers, and it will work wonders.

A second way to become free from self-consciousness is to see yourself as what you are: a representative of God Himself. In chapter 2, we discussed that a preacher is a herald and preaching is the proclamation of a message from the King. See yourself as an announcer of good news, a proclaimer of a message that is not your own, but from the throne of God Himself. These are not your words, they are His. See Him speaking through you. This is not self-aggrandizement; the one who delivers the message is not important, the message is what's important. By keeping your mind on the One who sent you, and on those to whom you were sent, you can find yourself forgetting yourself long enough to let God powerfully move through you as you preach.

Brooks's third point is *enjoyment of the work*. People who enjoy what they do are better at it than people who don't. This is a simple axiom that is nowhere more true than in preaching. I am surprised when I sometimes hear preachers say that preaching is the least favorite part of their ministries. "I love teaching!" or "I am a counselor at heart!" Maybe so, but I think all preachers should learn to love preaching. It should be the highpoint of their week. Everything else they do, and there are many things that fill a pastor's days, should take a back seat to preaching. Learn to love it, to look forward to it, to revel in it, and you will be more effective in the pulpit.

Why would a preacher not love to preach? I am not sure I can answer that. I have to confess; I did not want to be a preacher. I wasn't against it, I just had other plans: I wanted to be a scientist. I loved the Lord and served Him with all my heart, but I loved chemistry and physics, too. Among my greatest heroes were Faraday, Edison, Newton, and Galileo. But when God's call came to me, I gladly answered, and for forty-five years, I have had no regrets. There are aspects of the ministry I do not enjoy. When I pastored, there were things I was called upon to do that were not fun. But I have always loved preaching.

I think it may be that the egocentric dilettantes, the entertainment preachers, the pleasers, and the performers have given preaching such a bad name that some don't want to be identified with that sort of preaching. This unwillingness leads them to minimize the role that preaching plays in their ministries. They seem to be saying "Preaching is my duty, a part of what's required, but I don't love it; it's too shallow, too juvenile for me. I prefer the real meat of ministry." I get that. I understand why you would say that, but I have to tell you, you are wrong. Others may do it wrong and for the wrong reasons; they may exploit it or make an ego trip out of it, but preaching is still the highest calling of God given to humankind.

If you do not value preaching, or even if you simply don't enjoy it, those feelings will be communicated in many subtle ways to the congregation. People will follow strong leadership, they will like what you like and enjoy what you enjoy. If the preaching is the highlight of the service for you, it will be for them, too. This will pay rich dividends, not only for you, but for those who learn to love preaching through you.

Besides, if you don't love to preach, you would have been miserable on the pastoral staff at First Pentecostal Church of Jerusalem in AD 40. They gave themselves "continually to prayer, and to the ministry of the word" (Acts 6:4).

Next is *gravitas*. In his book *A Complete Guide to Sermon Delivery*, Al Fasol declares:

> Every congregation or audience need to know that the preacher or speaker is (1) a person of competence, a person "who knows what he is talking about;" (2) a person of integrity, a person who can be trusted, not a manipulator or exploiter; and (3) a person of vitality, a preacher who communicates a deep sense of belief in all that is said. The messenger's credibility with the congregation is critical in preaching.

How does a congregation know these things? By the way we behave ourselves. Silliness, foolishness, shallowness all destroy your ability to effectively preach the Word. I don't mean to equate gravitas with sternness or aloofness. You should be open, friendly, even fun to be with. Humor in the pulpit is not a no-no. But you can go too far and seem flighty, foolish, or shallow.

While we live in an ever more informal age, don't forget that dignity and decency must never be sacrificed to a misplaced desire to relate. Extreme clothing, over-the-top joking, and silly gestures rob a preacher of the gravitas that creates a level of comfort and trust in the congregation that is essential to effective preaching. You are an ambassador of the King of kings with a message from His lips, look and act like it.

Finally, Brooks lists *courage* as a source of power in preaching. The courage to preach is found in preaching the Word of God, regardless of whether it is popular. It is not found in harshness, arrogance, or anger while you are doing so. It is found in love. Loving people enough to preach what they don't want to hear takes real courage. You must not do it to show your imagined superiority, or to simply discharge your duty, but to compassionately try to persuade them to choose a better path, to strive to please God, or to repent and obey the gospel. This is your highest calling. It takes courage to show this kind of love, even at the risk of them leaving our congregations, speaking evil of us, or rejecting truth.

Sometimes, it isn't that people don't want to hear the more demanding truths of the Bible, it is because the values of the society we live in have seeped into their lives. They simply don't get what you are talking about; and what's worse, they seem to not even care if they get it. In "Turning an Audience into the Church," Will Willimon describes the "twin temptations" this modern attitude toward preaching offers preachers: you can "pander to their consumer mindset," or cynically "preach without expecting any significant change." In the first case you "avoid the controversial, even if it's biblical," and "strive to make people feel good." In the second you just discharge your duty and end up preaching powerless sermons because you expect no power can change those who hear them.

True courage will not allow you to fall for either of the twin temptations. True courage will demand that you see that even in a consumer and leisure-driven culture like ours, deep down, people are still hungry and hurting, they are still needy and wishing for something real and satisfying. The gospel still addresses these unchanging human longings. Willimon describes a period when he was teaching full time at Duke. During this time he was not pastoring and was attending a local church:

> One Sunday I walked into the church sanctuary and sat beside a middle-aged woman. . . . I asked how she was doing.
> "Not so well," she replied. "My husband was killed last week."
> "What?"
> "A drunk driver killed him," she continued. "What makes his death so hard is that we were separated at the time."
> "I'm so sorry." Taken back, I turned to greet an older man who had just sat down on the other side of me. "George, how have you been?" I asked.
> "I haven't been here in a month," he replied.
> "Anything wrong?"
> "Well, my mother died," he said. "It's just the worst that has ever happened to me. I miss her so much."
> "I'm so sorry to hear that." Just then the service began, for which I was extremely grateful.

I've never since presumed my listeners don't need and want the community created by the gospel.

Paul pointed out in his farewell to the Ephesian church that he had done what God had sent him to do in their city. "For I have not shunned to declare unto you all the counsel of God" (Acts 20:27). *Shunned* carries the meaning "cower or shrink." *Declare* in this context most likely means "preach." Paul is saying, "I had the courage to preach to you all that God gave me for you." May we all have the same testimony.

Interesting Preaching

Preaching boring sermons is inexcusable. When God gave us the Bible, He chose not to give us a dry, boring, theological textbook (well, except for some of those genealogies and ritual details). Instead He gave us an engaging, humorous, tear-jerking, tragic, bloody, beautiful, romantic, adventurous, puzzling, embarrassing, fascinating account of His efforts to covenant with humankind for more than four millennia. You can say these things and many more about the Bible, but you can't say it is boring. Why in the world then, would you content yourself to put your congregation to sleep when you have such a resource to preach from?

I have so far in this chapter warned you of the deadliness of distractions and showed you the pulpit demeanors that work; freedom from self-consciousness, enjoying what you are doing, gravitas, and courage. Now let's look at the basic building block of sermons: words. The right word in the right place demands attention from your audience like nothing else. Mark Twain said, "The difference between the right word, and the almost right word is the difference between lightning and the lightning bug." And he was right.

Words can inform us; they can also inspire us. Words can cause us to know more; they can also cause us to *be* more. The careful choice of words is vital to good preaching. Action verbs are better than passive. Gripping modifiers turn ordinary nouns into attention holders, and rhythm and cadence move your congregation toward the moment of decision. Used sparingly, even the much-ridiculed alliteration can make a phrase a memorable event.

Preaching is not writing because listening is not reading. There is no opportunity for the hearer to turn back a page or two to review what she missed while her mind wandered. Repetition is the only tool a preacher has to offer the hearer a chance to catch up. And while repetition is an effective tool, it is better to hold their attention in the first place. Attention cannot be demanded; it must be coaxed, carefully held, and nurtured, or it is lost. We accomplish these things by the use of dramatic imagery and memorable language. This is the power of well-chosen words.

Just as hammer and nails are the tools of the carpenter, words are the tools of the preacher. In communicating our thoughts, using the right tool for the job makes all the difference.

Consider this paragraph:

> From the stream in the middle of the field, five stones were chosen by David and placed in his pouch. When he saw David on the battlefield, Goliath was angered that such a young boy had been sent to fight him. David told the Philistine that he came, not trusting in weapons or skill, but in the name of the Lord. As Goliath rushed toward him, the shepherd boy took one of the stones, put it in his sling and flung it at the giant. It struck Goliath on the forehead and he fell to the ground. David cut off his head with his own sword and won the victory for his country and his God.

Not bad. The facts are there and the dramatic contrast between the inexperienced David and the trained killer Goliath is at least subtly communicated. Now let's punch it up a notch or two:

> David moved onto the battlefield with no sword, no spear, no armor; all he carried was a sling he had used since he was just a little boy. Goliath had still not noticed him when he crouched at the bank of the shallow stream that cut through the field and there carefully chose five stones, smooth and round. He placed them in his pouch and continued his advance toward his destiny. When Goliath saw the shepherd boy

he was incensed. "What am I, a dog," he roared toward the Israelite trenches "so you send a boy with a stick to run me home?"

David felt his own blood rise. "You come at me with a sword and a spear, but I come in the name of the Lord God of Israel!"

"Come on then," Goliath snarled, "I'll feed your carcass to the buzzards and the jackals!" As Goliath raced toward David, his massive sword whipping arcs through the air, the shepherd calmly reached in his pouch, put a stone in his sling and began to swing it around his head.

When the giant closed in, almost within reach of that massive sword, David released the stone. It flew straight and true, driving into Goliath's forehead, and the Philistine crashed to the ground. David ran to him, picked up his sword, and cut off his head. When David raised the grisly souvenir, the Philistine army ran for their lives.

That's better! But what makes it better? For one thing, it demands your attention by choosing more colorful and powerful words:

Instead of: From the stream in the middle of the field, five stones were chosen by David and placed in his pouch.

We have: Goliath had still not noticed him when he crouched at the bank of the shallow stream that cut through the field and there carefully chose five stones, smooth and round.

In the first sentence, we begin with three prepositional phrases: "from the stream," "in the middle," and "of the field," all modifiers, all dull. Next is a passive-voice verb and the subject being acted upon: "stones were chosen," also dull. The only action in the sentence is David "placed" the stones in his pouch.

By contrast, the second sentence is full of action: Goliath had (not) noticed. He (David) crouched, the stream cut, David chose. No passive verbs, and even the modifiers have been spiced up: "shallow" modifies "stream" both beginning with "s," and the five stones are modified by adjectives that come *after* it to add drama to them: "five stones, smooth and round."

Notice we added a sentence at the beginning to better capture the congregation's attention: David moved onto the battlefield with no sword, no spear, no armor; all he carried was a sling he had used since he was just a little boy. Look through and compare the rest of the two pieces, and you will find similar word choices that together make the second piece more dramatic, colorful, and interesting. Every word is chosen to convey a part of the story in a way that will gain and keep the interest of your hearers.

H. C. Brown and the other writers of *Steps to the Sermon*, in discussing style in the pulpit, say this: "Effective style is first of all, a matter of clarity." This is certainly true. Keep your words short and readily understandable. The children in the audience should understand what you are saying. But clarity need not be dull. Add a little hot sauce and you will make your audience *want* to hear what you have to say.

Sources Cited in Chapter 10

John A. Broadus, *On the Preparation and Delivery of Sermons*, 4th ed. (New York: Harper Collins, 1979).

Phillips Brooks, *Lectures On Preaching Delivered Before the Divinity School of Yale College in January and February, 1877* (New York: E. P. Dutton, 1878).

Al Fasol, A Complete Guide to Sermon Delivery (Nashville: Broadman & Holman, 1996).

Will Willimon, "Turning an Audience into the Church," in Haddon Robinson and Craig Brian Larson, eds., *The Art and Craft of Biblical Preaching* (Grand Rapids: Zondervan, 2005).

H. C. Brown, Jr., H. Gordon Clinard, Jesse J. Northcutt, *Steps to the Sermon* (Nashville: Broadman Press, 1963).

11

THE ANOINTING

> The writer seeks to change blood into ink; the preacher seeks to change ink into blood.
>
> Charles L. Bartow

> But ye have an unction from the Holy One.
>
> John, son of Zebedee

Preparing a purpose statement, using the emotional impact of our points, preserving the logic of our thoughts, choosing the right word, as well as all the other tools of public speaking we have discussed so far in this book, are essentially carnal techniques. Aside from the fact we are communicating the Word of God, the things we have studied in the last four chapters work for any type of public speaking. This is because, by trial and error, speakers over the past two and a half millennia have found these tools work simply because they touch human beings on a deep, almost subconscious level. And because they use basic human nature to produce results, they work for anybody, with any agenda. When asked how to make a speech, Winston Churchill answered in a style true to his form. Said he to his questioner, "If you have an important point to make, don't try to be subtle or clever. Use a pile driver. Hit the point once. Then come back and hit it again. Then hit it a third time—a tremendous whack." This, allowing for Churchill's colorful language and deft touch of sarcasm, is a perfect description of what we have studied in this book. These techniques have been used by great speakers for centuries. Churchill and Roosevelt used them. But so did Hitler, Mussolini, and Stalin.

What this means to us is that we must have something more than a mastery of technique. We must not fall prey, because of innate talent or acquired skill, to becoming cynical manipulators of the church and of the lost. We must not use cheap appeals to emotion: stories, illustrations, and questionable applications of biblical doctrines and texts, which may be dramatic, but are empty and totally disconnected from Scripture. We must not labor just to touch hearts without caring whether we have transformed them. This kind of preaching has robbed the church, discredited the calling, and even created a sense in saints and preachers alike that preaching is shallow, uninformed, and manipulative. We hear this in comments like, "We have enough meetings that only offer inspiration (read: preaching); we need teaching and practical tools more than inspiration!" I mean no disrespect for teaching and training; in fact, I am in favor of more of both. (That's why I wrote this book.) But we must not move preaching from the primary place it is given by Scripture, judging it unworthy to remain there.

We must not be manipulators but true men and women of God, committed to the Word of God, and to those who hear us preach. We must bring to them not carnality, but true spirituality. In this chapter, I will urge you, above all, to seek the anointing of the Spirit for your preaching.

Never be satisfied with anything less than the supernatural. Use the techniques we have studied for what they are: tools to make our preaching as effective as possible. But never forget they are not where our power is. Drench these tools in prayer and dedicate them to the use of the Holy Spirit. Do not trust in the tools, trust only in Him; only then will those who hear us not merely be moved, but changed.

It is difficult to describe the anointing; it is truly supernatural. Sometimes, the miracle happens and everything works. All the preparation, both of the sermon and your own heart, the worship that built the conducive atmosphere of the service, all of it comes together in a moment of unbelievable anointing. Most of the prose is yours, but you know you never could have written the music. The rhythms are from somewhere, someone else.

When you look down at your notes, they are alive. Nuances, whole revelations you did not see in your study, are now apparent and they come to your lips with an eloquence you could not have crafted in the quiet times. You are on fire. The deep is broken up and your own soul is exposed. The people who are hearing you are drawn in because you are drawn in; they are simply following you.

You are on a high wire, but you don't care. Some warning voice says you might say something foolish, but you ignore it. Another voice from deeper in the human side of you, maybe even a darker side, where there is frustration, disappointment, or even pride, tries to intrude with carnal words, even insulting or mean words, but you ignore them too. This is pure, this is truth, and it is coming from both you and Him, and this is preaching.

Getting to this place, allowing this to happen, is the highest goal of our calling. Here preaching is much more than speechifying, more than simply saying words, even words of eternal truth; here lives are changed, miracles happen, both in bodies and hearts. This preaching is what causes Felix to tremble, Festus to call out "Paul you are mad!" Agrippa to be almost persuaded, and the crowd at Pentecost to plead with Peter to tell them, "What must we do?" Getting here is what your life is about, this is where your life's work is accomplished.

She was talking about writing, but it's true of preaching too: Sophy Burnham says, "When it is going well, the words flow off your fingertips; you are immersed in the music. You could not possibly tell anyone what songs you

The Anointing

are hearing, what ecstasies you feel. 'I listen to the voices,' says Faulkner."

It isn't always like this, of course; sometimes you neither soar nor sing, you just slog. But when it *does* happen, there is nothing like it. How can we make it happen more? How can we enter this high place more frequently? We cannot manufacture this synergy with the Holy Spirit, we can only do those things that invite His coming, make ourselves available, and be able to recognize and seize the opportunity when it comes. Some of those things are simple, like getting enough rest so we are physically and emotionally engaged in the pulpit; others are harder, like leaving distractions behind, not preaching from our own pain, and for the moment truly forgetting ourselves.

Of course you must not be carried away from your study by this inspiration. I remember a well-known and very good preacher, who in the inspiration of the moment totally lost his audience and the service when he exuberantly expressed a "truth" that occurred to him on the spot but was patently false in scriptural terms, and everyone in the audience knew it. He spent months, even years, trying to explain that one away. Let the inspiration of the crowd and the anointing of the Spirit open your thought, inspire your language, engage your imagination, but always stay grounded in what you know to be so.

I am not talking about the rush that comes from a connection with an audience. Although remarkable, this is only a carnal, earthly thing. When a speaker transcends his arguments and truly inspires himself and his audience (e.g., *I have a dream! Ich bin ein Berliner! This was their finest hour! Mr. Gorbachev, tear down this wall!*), this synergy takes place. Abraham Lincoln's "lost speech" was delivered on May 29, 1856, at the Illinois State Republican Convention in Bloomington, and has been described as the greatest speech he ever gave. We don't know if it was or not because as Paul Angle writes: "So powerful was his eloquence that the reporters forgot to take notes of what he was saying. Several commenced, but in a few minutes they were entirely captured by the speaker's power, and their pencils were still." According to Robert Norton, about forty reporters were there but, like the audience of over one thousand, were "simply mesmerized."

"The audience sat enthralled," says Benjamin Thomas. "Men listened as though transfixed. Reporters forgot to use the pencils in their hands, so that no complete and authentic record of what may have been his greatest speech has ever been found. At the end, the hall rocked with applause."

This is what Aristotle meant when he spoke of emotionally engaging your hearers if you hope to persuade them that your arguments are true. This is public speaking at its finest and most effective. But it is not supernatural, it is not the anointing.

Preaching the Word of God is a spiritual occurrence. God uses the synergy between speaker and hearer to implant truth in the human heart, to move the needy to do that which can meet their need, and to save them that believe. He does this through His Spirit. This is what we call the anointing. A dead, dry presentation of even divine truth can leave the hearer cold and unresponsive, but the power of a true connection in the Spirit between the preacher and his congregation is the conduit through which the Spirit of God makes the Word live. Don't fear this anointing; it is at the heart of all great preaching. Learn to direct it, harness it. Don't lose yourself in the emotion it generates, but let that emotion give wings to your words and you will preach beyond your talent, your ability, and your skill.

If this anointing is the source of true power in preaching, do we need to bother with extensive notes, outlines, even fully written out portions of our sermons? Absolutely. The written notes from which we preach are not designed to stifle this inspiration of the moment, but to complement it. In fact, in my own experience, the more familiar I am with the facts, the biblical events, the scriptural basis of the sermon, the more likely it is the anointing will come. The comfort I feel when I have a good grasp of my message, and good notes to come back to regardless where the anointing may take me, liberates me to respond to the power of the anointing. When I am concentrating hard to simply remember exactly what it is I am trying to say, such as the points of the sermon, the illustrations, the flow of the arguments, and the facts that support all these, the less I am enraptured into the anointing. Notice, great preachers like Anthony Mangun and Mike Williams, who often read large segments of their sermons, but as the sermon progresses and the power of the presentation affects the audience, move into the anointing. You will see that when the anointing comes, it elevates the preacher, the sermon and the congregation into a higher realm. The same is true of other outstanding preachers like Wayne Huntley, Jack Cunningham, and Scott Graham. I witnessed it in great preachers of the past like C. M. Becton and J. T. Pugh. All these preachers and many, many others work, and worked hard to prepare their sermons, but always allowed the supernatural to break into their preaching.

The most brilliantly constructed, incredibly learned sermon is a waste of time, unless it is accompanied by the anointing. Seek the anointing, open your heart to it, allow it to move into the service. You don't have to finish the sermon, but you must have a move of God.

Was Paul For or Against?

I have sometimes been misunderstood when I speak on the Scripture passage that inspired the title for this book. Let's look at it again.

> For it is written, I will destroy the wisdom of the wise, and will bring to nothing the understanding of the prudent. Where is the wise? where is the scribe? where is the disputer of this world? hath not God made foolish the wisdom of this world? For after that in the wisdom of God the world by wisdom knew not God, it pleased God by the foolishness of preaching to save them that believe. For the Jews require a sign, and the Greeks seek after wisdom: But we preach Christ crucified, unto the Jews a stumblingblock, and unto the Greeks foolishness; But unto them which are called, both Jews and Greeks, Christ the power of God, and the wisdom of God (I Corinthians 1:19–24).

Duane Litfin, in his book *Paul's Theology of Preaching*, points out that the first four chapters of I Corinthians form a unique and enlightening accounting of Paul's concept of preaching: what it is, how it works, and what it does. Paul lays out for all time the primacy of preaching in the Christian life, and what makes it so important. In those chapters, he makes clear how preaching should be done.

In this passage from chapter 1, Paul contrasted competing interests in the life and role of the church: Jews want signs, Greeks want wisdom, but, Paul asserted, we preach. It is inescapable that Paul elevated preaching above the seeking of signs and the pursuit of wisdom. In fact, a less-than-careful reading might lead to the conclusion that Paul positioned preaching in place of the other two and thus excluded the pursuit of signs and wisdom from the Christian's life.

Because of this some have insisted that this means that Paul was against—to a greater or lesser degree—both the supernatural demonstration of the Spirit and the desire to study and seek education. When this passage is preached on, because of the passion this subject raises, unfortunately, that is what some hear. Depending on the individual's interests, this creates some confusion and not a little disagreement.

So it is important to rightly interpret Paul's stand on this important subject. What was Paul for and what was he against? As with all Scripture, this passage must be seen in context not only with its own surrounding verses, but with the entire corpus of Paul's writing. To believe that Paul was against learning is to ignore his advice to his young protégé,

Timothy: "Study to shew thyself approved unto God, a workman that needeth not to be ashamed, rightly dividing the word of truth" (II Timothy 2:15). Likewise, to assert that Paul in I Corinthians 1 set preaching in opposition to the supernatural, is to forget his statement to the same church in the same letter, in fact, only one chapter later: "And my speech and my preaching was not with enticing words of man's wisdom, but in demonstration of the Spirit and of power" (I Corinthians 2:4). This verse adds to the confusion and debate, because it has led some to believe Paul was against structured, planned sermons, especially those which use rhetorical persuasive techniques, and that he endorsed only demonstration of the supernatural!

How do we reconcile all this? It seems to me we must remember why Paul wrote these things. The apostle was trying to help a church that was filled with demonstration and power ("You come behind in no gift," he told them in 1:7), but struggled with carnality and competition. The people had come to regard preaching as some sort of competition, going so far as choosing which preacher they would root for: "I am of Paul!" "I am of Apollos!" 'I am of Cephas!" "I am of Christ!"

Paul was combating this divisive and carnal spirit by insisting that preaching is at the heart of what the church is, and everything else finds its place in relationship to preaching. He does not insist that preaching is all there is, he does not set up a competition between using rhetorical technique on the one hand, and supernatural demonstration on the other, with preaching in the middle. Rather, he acknowledges the role of all these things and connects them together. Preaching is more important than signs and the seeking of wisdom, but preaching contains both of these things, and is incomplete without them. For Paul it is a matter of emphasis. When he says, "The Jews seek signs, and the Greeks wisdom, *but* we preach," he is saying we value the essential aspects of the supernatural and wisdom, but for us, they find their place in the preaching of the gospel. It is the preaching of the gospel that we emphasize.

Then according to Paul, our sermons should be well-thought-out, the result of careful study of God's Word, and put together using the most effective tools possible. But when delivered, those sermons must be made alive by the presence of the supernatural; without the anointing they cannot possibly accomplish what they should. Anointed preaching should be accompanied by the demonstration of the power of God. Altar services, laying on of hands, healing lines, sweeping moves of God that prostrate human beings, bring tears and laughter, shouts and praises, ought not be rare or even occasional, they should be a consistent part of our preaching.

So what was Paul for, what was he against? Let me put it like this: Paul insisted that in contrast to the sign-seekers who hope to know God by following assumed supernatural manifestations and put their trust in them, and in contrast to the knowledge-seekers who hope to find God in the dry accumulation of knowledge and put their trust in wisdom, we preach. We preach with knowledge: faithful to the Word of God, rightly dividing it; but we also preach with anointing: the powerful, supernatural presence of God. By doing this, our trust rests, not with rhetorical technique, nor in superstition, but in God alone.

Where the Anointing Leads

The anointing has a purpose beyond inspiring the preacher and the congregation. When the Spirit moves into the sermon, it moves toward the goal of meeting the needs of those who are there. Sometimes the anointing will so move the congregation that they will simply not wait for you to finish. Be sensitive to both the people and the Holy Ghost, and quit! Several years ago, I was preaching at the Philippines General Conference. The crowds were huge. (I remember they said about ten thousand were there.) Preaching was a delight, even though I preached through an interpreter. The people were responsive, attentive, and the anointing was rich and powerful. One night, I had probably not been preaching more than ten minutes; I remember I was not even finished with the introduction, when there came a sweeping move of the Holy Spirit. Almost as one person, that great crowd surged to their feet and worshiped with all their hearts. As far as I could see, to the back rows of the balcony people were shouting, dancing, and praying. People were receiving the Holy Ghost everywhere. I encouraged it a while, then turned the service over to the service leader and joined in. Later, one of the national leaders thanked me for not preaching further, but letting the Spirit have its way. I thanked him. But what I wanted to say was, "What choice did I have? God took over!" I also wanted to say that I had learned what I know the hard way, by preaching away the move of God because I thought what I had to say was more important than what the Spirit was doing. I learned this is never the case.

Assuming the Spirit does not interrupt your message, as you begin the closing section you have so carefully crafted, make sure you are sensitive to what is happening in the congregation. Watch faces and body language. Are they ready to respond to the presence of God? Sometimes, one or two will come to the altar while you are still preaching; are they the exception, perhaps especially touched because of a situation in their life that has made them desperate for God? Or, is what they are feeling shared by many or even most of the congregation? If you see signs of emotion, hunger, and eagerness to respond to God throughout the crowd, it is time to stop preaching.

At the same time, be sensitive to the Spirit. What is God saying? How does He want you to conduct this climactic moment of the service? He knows every need of every person there. Let Him direct you in helping people break through doubt, push aside fear, and receive what they need.

Sometimes preachers ask me, "Do you give an altar call after every sermon?" The simple answer is yes. But let me qualify it by quoting Jonathan McClintock in his excellent book, *Life Preaching*: "Not every sermon will demand an altar call—in the traditional sense—but every sermon should lead to prayer. Whether you are wanting the people to decide to repent or rejoice, surrender or express faith, you will want them to call on the name of the Lord." Here is where you must be sensitive to the Spirit. What does God want to do?

Sometimes, I feel a prompting to emphasize the gift of the Holy Ghost. I will take a few moments and briefly describe what it is, how it is for everyone, and how to receive it. If I feel prompted, I will lead in a corporate repentance prayer, often I don't. Sometimes I will simply invite all who want the gift of the Holy Ghost to come forward first. Usually I will say something like, "If you come, someone will come with you, you won't be alone." This signals the saints to encourage those around them to come. Sometimes, after talking about the Holy Ghost, I will ask anyone who wants to receive the Holy Ghost to tell the person beside them, "I want the Holy Ghost." This does two things: it brings them to a decision by asking them to do something simpler than coming to the front and it commits the person to whom they speak to be part of the process. I then ask both to come to the front.

Sometimes I feel to emphasize healing or other areas of human need. If there is a possibility of embarrassment: marital problems, depression, financial problems, I will lump them together with other things like wanting a fresh touch of God, needing direction for your life, and so forth. It is important to mention these categories of need. An open-ended generic call to come pray is not nearly as effective as a focused call, as people will see themselves and their needs more clearly when they are named.

Sometimes, maybe most of the time, I do not feel to emphasize one particular need, but want everyone to come together. I still mention needs, tying them if possible to what I just preached. "The prodigal found the father waiting with open arms, God is waiting to welcome you!"

"The woman said if I may but touch the hem of his garment, I shall be whole! Come, you too can be whole!" "Those four lepers didn't wait for a better time, they knew there was no better time, they got up and went right then! Come now, now is the best time. Help is here now!"

You can still segment the appeal, that is, mention a need and urge them to come, then move on to another need.

At some point invite everybody. Make it clear the only requirement is need. "You are welcome to join us for a few moments of prayer to close our service. You don't have to be Pentecostal, you don't even have to be a Christian, or even religious; anyone can come. Come now, let's spend some time talking to the Lord."

Then join those who are praying. You will be tired and spent, but pray with people anyway. This is what all the study, thinking, and preparation was for. This is why you are a preacher, why Jesus came, why there is a Bible. This is what being a preacher means; to proclaim the gospel so that men, women, and children might be saved.

Sources Cited in Chapter 11

Winston Churchill on speechmaking: http://www.brainyquote.com/quotes/quotes/w/winstonchu111314.html

Sophy Burnham, *For Writers Only* (New York: Ballantine, 1994).

Paul M. Angle, ed., *The Lincoln Reader* (New Brunswick, NJ: Rutgers University Press, 1947).

Robert Norton, Abraham Lincoln Research Site, http://rogerjnorton.com/Lincoln2.html

Benjamin P. Thomas, *Abraham Lincoln, A Biography* (New York: Alfred A. Knopf, 1952).

Duane Litfin, *Paul's Theology of Preaching: The Apostle's Challenge to the Art of Persuasion in Ancient Corinth* (Downers Grove, IL: IVP Academic, 2015).

Jonathan McClintock, *Life Preaching* (Hazelwood, MO: Word Aflame Press, 2015).

Epilogue

Job sits in the ashes, "comforted" by his friends/accusers. There is a volcano of words, roaring, tumbling over one another. One cannot escape the impression of peacocks strutting, striving to impress, trying to outdo each other. Even Job in his own defense reaches for fine phrases and undertakes impressive verbal feats.

Now, at Job's insistent invitation, the Lord has arrived. Now, at last, the talkers fall silent as He speaks:

> Canst thou bind the sweet influences of Pleiades, or loose the bands of Orion? Canst thou bring forth Mazzaroth in his season? or canst thou guide Arcturus with his sons? Knowest thou the ordinances of heaven? canst thou set the

dominion thereof in the earth? Canst thou lift up thy voice to the clouds, that abundance of waters may cover thee? Canst thou send lightnings, that they may go, and say unto thee, Here we are? (Job 38:31–35).

God is showing Job and his friends the folly of their debate: they use many words, but are only wasting their time because they are making themselves to be experts in things they don't understand. And as far as making a difference, their words don't matter at all. There is no power in their words to change their circumstances, or anything else. To illustrate, He names three obvious areas where words fail:

> in commanding heavenly bodies
> in bringing rain
> in calling lightning from Heaven

No words, no matter how forceful, could accomplish those three things. But years after Job's time, the words of men would accomplish all three of these things.

Joshua spoke words, and the sun held in the zenith of the sky and the moon stood in the valley of Ajalon.

Elijah stopped the rain with mere words and three and a half years later he spoke, and the rains came again.

Elijah stood at the soaked-stone altar and called the lightning and it leapt to its feet and said: "Here I am!"

What is happening here? Was God wrong when He rebuked Job and his friends for their folly? Not at all. Not only the Law, but indeed all God's dealings with man were a schoolmaster, teaching us. Teaching is not an instantaneous process. Neither does the student stay at one level until the process ends; he or she learns and *puts to use that which is learned*.

God was, step-by-step, revealing the power of words, until the boundaries were brought down. Those things that were impossible in Job's time became possible in Joshua's and Elijah's. Words were gaining power.

But it did not stop.

Remember Ezekiel and the valley of dry bones? It was words, mere words, preached by a preacher to the unhearing remnants of a long-dead army that brought resurrection and life.

But it did not stop.

The Word was made flesh, and dwelt among us. All manner of diseases were healed, miracles were wrought. He declared if you *say* unto the mountain "Be removed!" it shall be removed. He said anything we *asked* in His name was possible.

But it did not stop.

Remember God's sobering description of the limitations of men's words to Job and his accusers? I said there were three, but there were actually four. The fourth could have had very little meaning to His hearers: "Knowest thou the ordinances of heaven? canst thou set the dominion thereof in the earth?" Now we understand more, because this limitation has no physical meaning, but a spiritual one. It was not in the power of words to do these things until death had been destroyed and salvation had come: "And I will give unto thee the keys of the kingdom of heaven: and whatsoever thou shalt bind on earth shall be bound in heaven: and whatsoever thou shalt loose on earth shall be loosed in heaven" (Matthew 16:19).

This is why preaching is the culmination of God's slow education of mankind. Thousands of years of God's careful planning, meticulous training, and patient instruction have reached their zenith in preaching the gospel. Limitations are gone. The answers to the great questions of time and eternity are found in the voices of men and women.

Now the words of a human being can affect eternity. Now we see the ultimate power of words: It pleased God through the foolishness of preaching to save. We do not save, but the preached gospel does. Now, because of the power of words, men and women can have eternal life.

No wonder Paul said we are the savor of life and death. In our voices is the very power of life and death over those who hear us. And who is sufficient for these things?

Acknowledgments

So many people offered encouragement and help along the way to the completion of this book, it would be impossible to list them all here. There are a few, however, to whom I am deeply indebted. To Dr. Robin Johnston, editor in chief of the United Pentecostal Church International and my friend, a constant encouragement who never missed an opportunity to remind me to persevere. To the staff of Word Aflame: the editors, graphic artists, and production staff. To David Johnson, who made it a better book. To Dr. David Norris, who encouraged me to write and helped improve the paper that formed the basis for chapters two and three. To Dr. Jeffrey Brickle, who taught me to love books even more than ever, and to not be afraid of Greek. To Tim Dugas and the staff at then Gateway College of

Evangelism who asked me to teach on preaching all those years ago. And my wife, Phyllis, always my First Reader and first editor, and the love of my life. And, finally, my grandson, Gavin, age seven, who though he felt on occasion that time spent writing took too much time away from playing, in the end announced that he was proud of Papa for writing this book. Thanks to all.

Bibliography

Achtemeier, Paul J. *Romans*. Interpretation: A Bible Commentary for Teaching and Preaching. Louisville: John Knox Press, 1985.

Ailes, Roger and Jon Kraushar. *You Are the Message: Secrets of the Master Communicators*. New York: Bantam Doubleday Dell, 1989.

Angle, Paul M., ed. *The Lincoln Reader*. New Brunswick, NJ: Rutgers University Press, 1947.

Barclay, William. *The Letter to the Romans*. Revised edition. Edinburgh: The Saint Andrews Press, 1975.

Bernard, David K. *The Apostolic Church in the Twenty-First Century.* Hazelwood, MO: Word Aflame Press, 2014.

———. *The Apostolic Life: Perspectives on Christian Living, Doctrine, and Ministry.* Hazelwood, MO: Word Aflame Press, 2006.

———. *Spiritual Leadership in the Twenty-First Century.* Hazelwood, MO: Word Aflame Press, 2015.

Blackwood, Andrew Watterson. *The Preparation of Sermons.* Nashville: Abingdon-Cokesbury, 1948.

Boreham, F. W. "Breaking the News" and "A Tangled Skein" in *Wisps of Wildfire.* London: Epworth Press, 1924.

Broadus, John A. *Lectures on the History of Preaching.* New York: Sheldon, 1886.

———. *On the Preparation and Delivery of Sermons.* Fourth edition. New York: Harper Collins, 1979.

Brooks, Phillips. *Lectures On Preaching Delivered Before the Divinity School of Yale College in January and February, 1877.* New York: E. P. Dutton, 1878.

Brown, H. C., Jr., H. Gordon Clinard, Jesse J. Northcutt. *Steps to the Sermon.* Nashville: Broadman Press, 1963.

Burnham, Sophy. *For Writers Only*. New York: Ballantine, 1994.

Carson, D. A., R. T. France, J. A. Motyer, and G. J. Wenham, eds. *New Bible Commentary: 21st Century Edition*. 4th ed. Leicester, England; Downers Grove, IL: InterVarsity Press, 1994.

Chambers, Stanley. "Can the United Pentecostal Church Survive the Onslaught of History?" Preached at the General Conference of the United Pentecostal Church International in 1967.

Chappell, Clovis. "A Good Man's Hell." In *Sermons on Biblical Characters*. Garden City, NY: Doubleday Doran, 1928.

———. "The Woman of the Shattered Romances." In *Sermons on Biblical Characters*.

Dargan, E. C. *A History of Preaching*. New York: George H. Doran Co., 1905.

Demaray, Donald E. *An Introduction to Homiletics*. Grand Rapids: Baker, 1974.

Dewey, Joanna. "Textuality in an Oral Culture: A Survey of the Pauline Traditions." In *Orality and Textuality in Early Christian Literature*, edited by Joanna Dewey and Elizabeth Struthers Malbon. Atlanta: Scholars Press, 1994.

Edwards, Johnathan. "Sinners In the Hands of an Angry God." Available from several online sources. http://www.jonathan-edwards.org/Sinners.html. Accessed July 30, 2016.

Fasol, Al. *A Complete Guide to Sermon Delivery.* Nashville: Broadman & Holman, 1996.

Friedrich, Wolfgang. "Preaching." In *Theological Dictionary of the New Testament,* edited by Gerhard Kittel and Gerhard Friedrich; translated by Geoffrey W. Bromiley. Grand Rapids: Eerdmans, 1964–76.

Gossip, Arthur John. "What Christ Does for a Soul." In *From the Edge Of the Crowd.* Edinburgh: T & T Clark, 1924.

Guidroz, V. A. "The Death March." https://www.pentecostalherald.com/articles/article/old-sermons-still-live-preaching-vily-able-guidroz. Accessed July 30, 2016.

Hall, J. L. and David K. Bernard, eds. *The Pentecostal Minister.* Hazelwood, MO: Word Aflame Press, 1991.

Hersey, John. *Hiroshima.* New York: Alfred A. Knopf, 1946.

Jones, Jerry. "Knowing Where to Run." In *Amnon Had a Friend and Other Sermons.* Hazelwood, MO: Word Aflame, 2006.

Jordan, J. Mark. *Living and Leading in Ministry*. Hazelwood, MO: Word Aflame Press, 2006.

Kesler, Jay. "Overfed, Underchallenged." In *The Art and Craft of Biblical Preaching*, edited by Haddon Robinson and Craig Brian Larson. Grand Rapids: Zondervan, 2005.

Lange, John Peter, Philip Schaff, F. R. Fay, and M. B. Riddle; J. F. Hurst, tr. *A Commentary on the Holy Scriptures: Romans*. Bellingham, WA: Logos Bible Software, 2008.

Larsen, David L. *The Company of the Preachers: A History of Biblical Preaching from the Old Testament to the Modern Era*. Grand Rapids: Kregel Academic & Professional, 1998.

Litfin, Duane. *Paul's Theology of Preaching: The Apostle's Challenge to the Art of Persuasion in Ancient Corinth*. Downers Grove, IL: IVP Academic, 2015.

Masefield, John. "Truth." In *The Story of a Round House and Other Poems*. New York: MacMillan, 1912.

McClintock, Jonathan. *Life Preaching*. Hazelwood, MO: Word Aflame Press, 2015.

Norton, Robert. Abraham Lincoln Research Site, http://rogerjnorton.com/Lincoln2.html. Accessed July 30, 2016.

Pitt-Watson, Ian. "Lifeblood of Preaching." In *The Art and Craft of Biblical Preaching*.

Pollan, Michael. *A Place of My Own: The Education of an Amateur Builder*. New York: Bantam Doubleday Dell, 1997.

Robinson, Haddon and Craig Brian Larson, eds. *The Art and Craft of Biblical Preaching*. Grand Rapids: Zondervan, 2005.

Runia, Klaas. "What is Preaching According to the New Testament?" The Tyndale Biblical Theology Lecture for 1976, delivered at the School of Oriental and African Studies, London, on January 4th, 1977.

Sangster, William E. *The Craft of Sermon Construction*. Philadelphia: Westminster Press, 1950, 1951.

Sangster, William. *The Approach to Preaching*. London: Epworth Press, 1951. Reprinted. Grand Rapids: Baker, 1974.

Sproul, R. C. *The Gospel of God: An Exposition of Romans*. Great Britain: Christian Focus Publications, 1994.

Spurgeon, Charles H. "The Stone Rolled Away." In *Twelve Sermons on the Resurrection*. Grand Rapids: Baker, 1968.

BIBLIOGRAPHY

Stitzinger, James F. "The History of Expository Preaching." In *Rediscovering Expository Preaching*, edited by John McArthur, Jr., Richard L. Mayhue, and Robert L. Thomas. Dallas: Word Publishing, 1992.

Stott, John R. W. "A Definition of Biblical Preaching." In *The Art and Craft of Biblical Preaching*.

Stott, John R.W. *Between Two Worlds*. Grand Rapids: Eerdmans, 1982.

Thomas, Benjamin P. *Abraham Lincoln, A Biography*. New York: Alfred A. Knopf, 1952.

Warren, Rick. "The Purpose-Driven Title." In *The Art and Craft of Biblical Preaching*.

Wiersbe, Warren W. *The Bible Exposition Commentary*. Wheaton, IL: Victor Books, 1996.

Willimon, Will. "Turning an Audience into the Church." In *The Art and Craft of Biblical Preaching*.

Yaghjian, Lucretia. "Ancient Reading." In *The Social Sciences and New Testament Interpretation*, edited by Richard Rohrbaugh. Peabody, MA: Hendrickson, 1996.

Printed in Great Britain
by Amazon